Adopting a Daughter from China

Denise Harris Hoppenhauer

iUniverse, Inc.
New York Lincoln Shanghai

Adopting a Daughter from China

iUniverse books may be ordered through booksellers or by contacting:

iUniverse
2021 Pine Lake Road, Suite 100
Lincoln, NE 68512
www.iuniverse.com
1-800-Authors (1-800-288-4677)

Because each adopted child's circumstances are unique, the guidelines offered here may not be appropriate for some children.

ISBN-13: 978-0-595-41523-6 (pbk)
ISBN-13: 978-0-595-85872-9 (ebk)
ISBN-10: 0-595-41523-7 (pbk)
ISBN-10: 0-595-85872-4 (ebk)

Printed in the United States of America

For my children,

Callie and Sean

And the millions of children,
waiting for a family to call thier own.

Contents

Foreword

One of the most fascinating things about building a family through adoption is that where we start out at is often not where we end up. For our first child, we were leaning towards a boy, we adopted a girl. We were thinking baby; our daughter was a three-year-old toddler. We wanted the perfect child. Okay—she is perfect-for me, she just happens to have had a cleft lip and palate.

Whether you are a family who experiences infertility or one with biological children, I firmly believe that the child that is supposed to be yours will be. This most entrusted gift from God has been pre-ordained to be your destiny, your heart, the very essence of your being.

For the Chinese, the proverb of the Red Thread affirms these beliefs.

"An invisible red thread connects those destined to meet, regardless of time, place, or circumstance. The thread may stretch or tangle, but it will never break."

After I wrote *Adopting A Toddler*, I had no plans to write a second adoption book. but as we know the threads that bind us may have other plans. Plans that we may not recognize for what they are.

First, I stumbled across a copy of *Lost Daughter's of China* at an outlet bookstore, so inexpensive that I couldn't resist. Not yet realizing the forces that were at play, these forces lead me to begin working with a Chinese adoption program. The threads twisted and turned, and occasionally I would receive e-mail from pre-adoptive China families who had purchased *Adopting A Toddler*. Finally, I realized they needed a book of their own.

And who knows where the threads may lead me? One can only wait and see. Perhaps one day, it will lead me to China.

Chapter 1

Adopting From China

The People's Republic of China

Before you travel to the People's Republic of China to adopt your child, it is important to have a basic understanding of China, it's people, culture, history and how they influence modern day China. As a prerequisite, this will help you prepare for this journey of a "lifetime." No longer will your family be American, or European descent, but Chinese as well. When you adopt and embrace a child from China, you in turn will be adopted by China.

Cultural Identity

Most adoptions from China are trans-racial adoptions: Caucasian parents adopting an Asian child. Adoptive parents must assume the responsibility of fostering cultural identity. Parents must nurture their child's cultural heritage and recognize the importance of their birth country. For children who have no birthparent history this is especially important. The Birth country becomes in a sense a "surrogate" birthmother.

Adoptive parent's opinions, attitudes, and perception of China will build the foundation for a positive cultural identity in their child. Acknowledging differences in the two cultures. Adding too, rather than taking away from one to give to another. Learning specific skills such as language is less likely to be beneficial to your daughter than the overall perceptions of China that she receives from you. The celebration and acknowledgment of cultural differences will help enhance and empower her as an individual.

Just as you will never be Chinese/Asian, your daughter will never be Caucasian. It is important for your child to identify with both cultures. Acknowledgment of culture is important to your daughter's adjustment and

1

personal identity. While cultural competency would be almost impossible for your daughter to achieve without being raised within the environment, you can raise her with a strong personal identity, who possesses knowledge of Chinese culture, beliefs and values.

Adoption from China

In the last five years alone, more than 31,000 children have been adopted from the People's Republic of China by United States Citizens.

2005	7,906
2004	7,044
2003	6,859
2002	5,053
2001	4,681

Approximately 97% were infant and toddler girls. The majority are under the age of two. One estimate is that there nearly 1 million children, mostly girls live in orphanages or in Foster Care China. Socio-economic based government restrictions along with thousands of years of cultural tradition and gender inequality all play a role.

What is commonly called the one child policy allows families 1 son or 2 children. If the first child is a girl, the family can try again for a son. The policy is less enforced in rural areas than in urban ones and many minority groups are exempt in an effort to promote cultural preservation. While this policy was originally designed to help lower birth rates and child abandonment, it has been ineffective.

While it may appear at first glance that the people of China care little for their children, that is not the case. The majority of Chinese people care greatly about their children and do not agree or condone child abandonment. However thousands of years of cultural tradition are hard to overcome: especially in a society where sons carry on the family name and care for their parents in old age. When a daughter marries, she becomes a member of her husband's family and is responsible for her in-laws.

Families can not place children for adoption or openly place them at an orphanage. Other family members must care for children, whose parents are deceased. Therefore the vast majority of children in Chinese orphanages are true abandonment cases. Parents who have abandoned their children believe that this is their only option.

Most babies who are abandoned are healthy girls under the age of 1-month-old who are 2nd and 3rd born daughters. Boys and girls who have special needs: cleft lip and palate, albinism, or other birth defects are also abandoned by their birth parents. Very little information about abandoned children is available, as it is illegal to abandon a child in China. Most birthparents are rarely identified or subsequently prosecuted.

Very little is known about the child other than the date and location of where she was found. An estimated birth date is given based on the baby's umbilical cord. On occasion the birth date or first name may be pinned to a child's blanket or she may have a special memento left with her. Typically no medical or social history is available.

Recent changes in Chinese law allows families to pay a fine for having more than one child as opposed to the harsher penalties of the past. Because of this many more Chinese families will not abandon their children. Currently only a limited number of orphanages place children for adoption. In the future, adoptive families may have to travel to more remote areas as a result of these changes and the availability of adoptable children.

Other factors that may significantly impact international adoption from China are that a Chinese family can now adopt an abandoned child if they have fostered the child for a certain amount of time. The culture of having a male child first is diminishing. More people, especially those in the countryside, accept whatever children they have. The Chinese people do not condone child abandonment and improvements in gender equality allow women to earn the same income in the cities.

The China Center for Adoption Affairs (CCAA)

In June of 2006, The China Center for Adoption Affairs celebrated its 10th Anniversary. Since it's inception more than 50,000 Chinese children have found homes in the U.S. The CCAA is responsible for all activities related to international and domestic adoption. It receives and reviews adoption applications and other adoption related documents from foreign adoption agencies.

The CCAA's responsibilities include acting as a foreign policy consultant for adoption affairs, locating and assessing potential adoptees for verification that they have meet the requirements of the "Adoption Law of the People's Republic of China" and are eligible for adoption, approving adoption applications, and matching chidlren with adoptive families.

Additionally, the CCAA verifies qualifications and assesses the practices of foreign adoption agencies, is responsible for archives and record keeping of adoption documents, the follow up of adopted children through post placement reports, and other actives related to the well being of Chinese children who are under their supervision and reside in orphanages known as Social Welfare Institutes. For more information about the China Center for Adoption Affairs, see: www.China-CCAA.org

Chinese Adoption Terminology and Acronyms

DTC	Dossier to China
LID	The date the Dossier is logged in by/at the CCAA
SN	Special Needs Child
NSN	Non-special Needs Child
WC	Waiting Child
LOI	Letter of Intent-letter sent to the CCAA to request to adopt a specific child.
PA	Pre-approval—CCAA approved you to adopt a specific child and you are officially matched with her.
DOPA	Date of PA
TA	Final approval to travel to adopt from China
DOTA	Date of TA
DOT	Date of Travel

China Today

The origins of present day China date back to 3000 BC. The capital city Beijing (formerly Peking) dates back to the 12th century BC. It is the political, economic and cultural center of the country. It is a large metropolitan city and a hub for international business and travel. Beijing Capital International Airport is about a 40-minute ride from the city center. Beijing boasts a population of over 12 million people. China's population is over 1.3 billion.

In China there are fifty-six ethnic minority groups: Including Tibetans, Uighures, and Mongolians. The standard language (The only one used approved for use by the media.) is Mandarin Chinese, which is known as the putongha or the "common tongue." There are seven main dialects spoken by ethnic minorities. Cantonese is the second most common language spoken in China. While most people speak Mandarin, Cantonese is commonly spoken in the city of Guangzhou. There are also high and low dialects that are a key indicator of local identity in both the Mandarin and Cantonese language.

The Mandarin Chinese language is spoken with sounds called Tones. There are very few syllables spoken in Chinese: approximately 400 versus 12,000 in English. Tones help the small number of syllables to multiply and assist in alleviating the problem. Words with the same sound express different meanings.

The written language is called Pinyin. Although the term is not entirely accurate, it is commonly called calligraphy. As a written language is very difficult to learn as the Chinese characters represent words and meaning phonetically and each tone must be carefully applied.

The Geography of China

China is a diverse country. It encompasses everything from large cities with wealthy business owners to rural farmlands where poor farmers struggle to survive. The geography includes deserts, mountains, coastal areas and fertile river basins. Dry seasons and monsoons dominate its weather. Eastern areas of China have hot, wet summers. Most rainfall in China occurs during the monsoon season of May through October.

China has many lakes and rivers. Rivers in China are of significant importance to both transportation and irrigation of farmlands. The Chang Jiang (Yangtze River) River is the longest/largest in China and the third longest river in the world, behind the Nile and the Amazon. It divides North and South China. Almost 95% of people in China live in the Northern and Southern regions. The remaining 5 percent are mostly ethnic groups, which occupy the Northwest and Qinghai-Tibetan areas. There are distinct customs and lifestyles associated with the geography of the four regions of China.

Two thirds of the country consist of mountain ranges and many of the world's tallest mountains are located within China. The region of Western China encompasses the Himalayan, Tian, and Pamir Mountain ranges.

North China has a short hot summer with long, very cold winters. The fourth longest river in the world, the Huang He (Yellow River) River is located in Northern China. It is know as "China's Sorrow" because of the flooding that has occurred throughout history. It continues to be a challenge for the Chinese people as flooding, serious erosion, and droughts occur along the riverbanks, which effect approximately 100 million people.

Southern China has a warmer, more fertile climate with long summers that allow time for several crops. Rice is the most important and is grown in Southern and Central China. Other major food crops are corn, peanuts, soybeans, sugar cane, tea, and wheat.

China has many natural resources including coal, copper, gold, mercury, uranium zinc, and rich oil reserves.

For coastal areas such as Guangzhou, typhoon season is between July and September. A typical typhoon season averages about five typhoons. Fishermen catch a variety of saltwater fish including sturgeon, crabs, eel, herring, and sharks. China uses large ponds to evaporate seawater and is second to the US in salt production.

Famous Sights in China

Some of China's earliest; great inventions include the abacus, acupuncture, cast iron, chopsticks, the compass, gunpowder, papermaking and printing. Other Chinese inventions include the game chess, decimal mathematics, paper-money, modern agriculture, umbrellas, and the wheelbarrow.

The city of Beijing is famous for its long history and rich culture. With its beautiful gardens, Great Wall, museums, palaces, and temples, many of the most famous and culturally significant places in China are located in and around Beijing:

Tian'anmen Square—"the Gate to Heavenly Peace" A national symbol to China, it is to China what Red Square is to Russia. Covering 122 acre, many ceremonies and demonstrations have been held at Tian'anmen over the last hundred years. One of the most important of these was the declaration of the People's Republic of China in 1949.

Surrounding the square is the Great Hall of the People, Museum of Chinese History, and the Museum of Chinese Revolution. In addition the Mao Zedong Mausoleum, the Qianmen Gate and the entrance to the Forbidden City.

The Forbidden City—Located at Tian' anmen Square, it is the world's largest palace complex with 9,999 buildings and over 700,000 square meters of floor space. It consists of an Outer court where Chinese Emperors ruled the country and the Inner court where the royal family lived. The predominate color is yellow: to signify the royal family. Today it houses many rare antiques, paintings and many fine examples of royal architecture. It is open to the public.

The Temple of Heaven—The Chinese Emperor was known as the "Son of Heaven." The Temple of Heaven, one of Beijing's most famous landmarks because of it architectural design, was built for the emperor to show respect, hold ceremonies, worship heaven, and to pray for good harvest.

The Summer Palace—Known in China as "Yiheyuan" or Garden of Nurtured Harmony. The Summer Palace located in the Haidian District in the outskirts of Beijing is home to one of the most noted gardens in the world.

On the grounds of the Summer Palace is the Marble Boat, a two-story pavilion built of marble on the order of the Empress Dowager Cixi in 1893. Some historians believe her power actually surpassed that of England's Queen Victoria, a contemporary.

The Great Wall of China—A defensive wall built to protect from invaders is almost 3000 miles long. The great wall is so large that is on of the few objects visible from space and is a must see or visitors to China.

The Ming Tombs—Located about 50 kilometers northwest of Beijing, in a valley to the south of Tianshou Mountain, thirteen out of the sixteen Ming emperors are buried here. The tombs were built by the 13th Ming Emperor and used from the 14th to 17th Century.

Classic Chinese Opera—Also called Beijing Opera, was originally performed for the royal court and later became a public form of entertainment. Traditional Beijing Opera consist of over one thousand works based mainly on history, traditional and politics. There are four main roles:

> Sheng—chief, main male role
>
> Jing—male with colorful painted face
>
> Chou—clown role
>
> Dan—female role

Chinese Acrobats—Acrobats first began performing in 500 BC Much of Chinese acrobatics includes delicate balancing acts, contortions and juggling. No circus would be complete without them.

Terra Cotta Warriors—Located in the Shaanxi province—Over 7,000 pottery soldiers, horses, chariots, and weapons dating back over 2,000 years ago to the

Qin Dynasty have been unearthed in Xian. The Museum of Qin Terra Cotta Warriors and is filled with these life size terracotta figures of warriors and horses arranged in battle formations.

Chinese Holidays and Other Important Dates

The celebrations of Chinese Holidays and Events may effect your travel plans. The U.S. Embassy in Guangzhou may be closed on both Chinese and American holidays. In addition you may find local events that you may attend while you are in the adoption process or after you have completed your adoption.

Chinese New Year—It is the largest and most celebrated holiday of the year. The actual date varies and is determined by the lunar calendar but is usually held sometime between late January and mid February. Besides celebrating the New Year, it is also a time to remember deceased family members.

Preparations for Chinese New Year includes buying presents for one another, purchasing new clothes and cleaning the house to make way for good luck. Doors and windows may be painted red and red and gold decorations are used. The red represents good luck and the gold represents wealth.

During the Chinese New Year celebration children receive lucky red money packs called "Hong Bao" which contain candy and small coins. There are many parties and events, which may continue for several days after. Firecrackers are meant to scare off evil spirits as are the *Lion Dancers* frequently seen during the New Years celebration.

The Lantern Festival—On the fifteenth day of the New Years Celebration. Lucky red lanterns of all shapes and sizes are placed everywhere for decoration. Lantern exhibits, lion and dragon dances: which symbolize good fortune and power, and eating Tang Yuan; rice dumplings with stuffing, characterize this popular celebration. The Lantern Festival also marks the end of the Chinese New Year season.

Qing Ming—The Clear and Brightness Festival is usually held around April 4-6, or 106 days following the winter solstice. It's a traditional belief that a person's good fortune is linked to the happiness of one's ancestral spirits. Cleaning up ancestors' tombs and acknowledging the dead is a major event.

The Spring Trade Fair—Usually held during the last two weeks of April, in Guangzhou, the Spring Trade Fair may require you to delay travel during this time. It is required that you visit the U.S. Embassy in Guangzhou, and when the trade fair is in town it may be extremely difficult to find a hotel.

May Day-May 1-2 International Labor Day Holiday sometimes called Chinese National Holiday. Employees enjoy a paid day-off.

Dragon Boat Festival—The Chinese patriot Festival is called Duan Wu Jie in Chinese. Jie means festival. The festival is celebrated on the 5th day of the fifth month of the Chinese lunar calendar. The origins of the festival are believed to be derived from the commemoration of a great patriot and poet Qu Yuan. Qu Yuan served in the court of Emperor Huai during the Warring States (475–221 BC). He was a wise and fought against corruption. Eventually he was exiled. During his exile, he traveled extensively, taught and wrote about his ideas. Eventually he ended his life by flinging himself into the Miluo River.

After people heard he drowned, Fishermen went in their boats to search for his body. People threw food into the river to the feed fish, in hopes of finding his body. From that time on, people started to commemorate Qu Yuan on the anniversary of his death, through dragon boat races and eating zongzi. This dumpling, which comes in different shapes and fillings, is the most popular food for the festival.

Children's Day (June 1) A Favorite for Chinese children. Many movie theaters, parks and museums, etc. are open free to children. Elementary schools throw parties and parents often buy children presents.

Mid-Autumn Festival—Moon Festival-Lunar Festival—The Chinese Moon Festival is on the 15th day of the 8th lunar month. It is second only to the Chinese New Year in significance. The moon on this day is the fullest and largest to the eye. Legends of fairies, goddesses, and star-crossed lovers abound about the Moon Festival. Viewing the moon while feasting on moon-cakes and drinking wine are a highlight of this nighttime event.

National Liberation Day—October1-2—It is the anniversary of the founding of the People's Republic of China in 1949. The victory celebration commemorates the Chinese Communist Forces; under Mao Zedong, over the Nationalist Forces. Celebrations usually include parties and fireworks. Employees receive two paid days off.

The Fall Trade Fair—Much like the Spring Trade Fair, the Fall Trade fair is held during the last two weeks of October. The Fall Trade Fair may require you to delay adoption travel to Guangzhou during this time.

Chinese Zodiac

In tradtional China a rotating cycle of the twelve animal signs was a folk method used for naming the years. These signs represent a cyclical concept of time. The Chinese Lunar Calendar is based on the cycles of the moon. The beginning of the year falls somewhere between late January and early February in the Chinese calendar. The Chinese adopted the Western calendar in 1911, but still use the lunar calendar for festive occasions such as the Chinese New Year. Chinese calendars often print the solar dates of the Western calendar and the Chinese lunar dates.

In Chinese folklore horoscopes developed around the animal signs. For example, a Chinese horoscope may predict that a person born in a certain year will have specific traits or characteristics, much like the monthly western horoscope. In the Chinese calendar, every year is assigned an animal name or "sign" according to a repeating cycle: Rat, Ox, Tiger, Rabbit, Dragon, Snake, Horse, Sheep, Monkey, Rooster, Dog, and Boar. Every twelve years the same animal "sign" reappears.

According to Chinese legend, the animals quarreled about who was to head the cycle of years. The gods were called to intervene and decided the animals should race to the opposite side of a riverbank to see who would be first. The animals would receive their years according to their finish. As the race began, the Rat, unbeknownst to the Ox, jumped upon his back to cross the river. As the Ox neared the finish line, the Rat jumped off his back and won the race. Because he was lazy, the Pig finished last. This why the Rat is the first year animal in the cycle, the Ox is the second and the Pig last.

Calendar Years

2000	The Year of the Dragon
2001	The Year of the Snake
2002	The Year of the Horse
2003	The Year of the Goat
2004	The Year of the Money
2005	The Year of the Rooster

2006	The Year of the Dog
2007	The Year of the Pig
2008	The Year of the Rat
2009	The Year of the Ox or Buffalo
2010	The Year of the Tiger
2011	The Year of the Rabbit

Chinese Taboos

In China, white is the color of morning. Never give anyone white flowers as a gift. Flowers should be given in odd numbers and never give four to anyone. The number 4 is associated with death. Some buildings actually have no fourth floor. They skip from number 3 to number 5. Avoid talking about politics, religion, human rights, and women's issues.

The Chinese Government

In 1949 the Chinese People's Political Conference was held in Beijing and drafted the current provisional constitution. The Chines government is lead by the President and Party Secretary, the Premier and the National People's Congress Chairman of Standing Committee.

The State socialist system is comprised of two parts.

1. Democracy is practiced within the ranks of the people.
2. Dictatorship is practiced over enemies of the state.

The people manage the economic, cultural and social aspects of government and the state overseas any disruption of the people's democracy.

Education in China

China has one of the highest literacy rates in the world. Almost 98% of school age children attend school. School is year round. Primary education is required but children in rural areas may or may not attend school. Primary school lasts six years.

Middle school also lasts six years. Children may attend regular middle and high school or secondary vocational educational programs. These typically last three to five years and primarily train skilled workers and technicians.

Vocational schools train engineers, agricultural, medical, and educational professionals and many other specialized professionals.

Graduates are not assigned jobs by the government and may apply for a university education. Most do not attend college and only about 10% apply. Competition is strong and only about 25% of applicants are accepted. Only a small number of universities in China offer a Masters or Doctorate degree.

Currency

The main bank in China is the People's Bank of China. They set the value/ exchange rate for money. The currency in China is the Renminbi. The unit is the Yuan. Smaller units are jico and fen.

> 10 fen = 1 jico
>
> 10 jico = Yuan
>
> 1Yuan = approximately 0.12457 U.S. Dollars
>
> 1 U.S. Dollars = approximately 8.02757 in Chinese Yuan
>
> 10$U.S. Dollars = approximately 80.2757 in Chinese Yuan

Chapter 2

What's in a Name?

Naming Your Child

One of the most important things an adoptive parent is asked to do after they decide to adopt a child is to choose a name. This is a very personal decision and helps create an instant bond with your child. No longer a nameless, faceless little person, your new addition now has a name by which she will become known.

Naming your child is often a difficult decision. Many people plan and think about names for their children for a long time; they may have already chosen special family names or ones that they like. A key difference in choosing names for an older infant or toddler is that she will already have a name that she is known by and responds to.

In most cases, when you receive the referral for your daughter, you will be given medical and developmental information, social history, and a small picture along with her Chinese name. Many people struggle with how to change or keep their daughter's Chinese name. Some of the factors that must be considered are her age, cultural ties, and the complexity of her existing name.

Most often families are asked to select a name after they receive a referral but before they travel to complete the adoption. On occasion agencies may ask families to select a name before they receive a referral or shortly after arrival in China. If you have not been asked to select your daughter's name before travel, it is a good idea to have one picked out by the time you land in Beijing.

Cultural Considerations

A common misconception is that a child's name may have been chosen by her birth parents and thus deserves special consideration. This is not usually the case, especially when children are abandoned at a young age. On the rare occasion that a birthparent leaves a child's name on a note, the orphanage may or may not use that name.

Instead, orphanage workers, adoption professionals, or government officials may have named your daughter. Children in orphanages may have been given the same last name as the orphanage director, town, mayor, or other area celebrities. Sometimes all children in an orphanage may be given the same middle or last name, or a variation of the name so that they share a common connection.

Even more perplexing is that the child's legal name may not be the name one that she goes by. She may be called a derivative of the name, a nickname, or another name that someone else may have chosen.

Names usually have meaning, and each child will have three names a surname, a generational name and a personal, or first name. Your daughter's name may in someway incorporate where she was found, what the season of her birth was, or reflect her personality. Children are commonly called by their whole name. Repeating a child's first name or the last syllable of a middle name two times is a common nickname.

Cultural considerations help foster a child's heritage. These considerations may be especially important to help maintain the cultural identity of a child who is of a different ethnic heritage than her adoptive parents. Keeping at least part of a child's given name can help provide an important link between her birth country and her adopted country. This may not seem important to a child when she is younger, but it most likely will be as she comes to understand adoption and her origins.

Other factors to consider include whether the name is impossible to pronounce correctly, whether the child will be teased about her name, and whether the name is socially acceptable in your community. Because words mean different things in different languages, it may be that your daughter's given name has a completely different meaning, which may necessitate a name change. One word of caution, it is not usually recommended to select a new Chinese name for your daughter without assistance from someone who is fluent in Chinese.

Incorporating a Name

Your child's age should be one of the greatest factors in deciding how to incorporate a new name. The younger a child is, the easier it will be for her to adjust to a new name, while an older toddler may be more resistant to change. Her name may be the only thing that truly belonged to her, and she may be reluctant to let go. It is who she is: her personal identity.

Deborah McCurdy, adoption supervisor with Beacon Adoption Center in Great Barrington, Massachusetts, advises that "many adoption workers and psychologists feel if your child is age two or over, it is vitally important to call him by the name he is accustomed to, at least until he is ready to make the major change on his own."

Frequently, families decide to give their daughter a new first name and keep her Chinese name as a middle name. By keeping a name that identifies your child with her culture, you are providing her with the opportunity to affirm her cultural identity.

Another option would be to anglicize the child's given name to a similar name or a translation of the given name. Masculine and feminine forms of names may be worth considering as well.

Making the Transition

The use of a new name together with a child's given name can help ease the transition from one to the other, even if you have decided not to keep the given name and have changed both names. The theory is that as your child gets used to being called by her new name, you can start dropping the use of the old name. As your daughter is adjusting to name changes, it is important to use positive reinforcement to teach your daughter to use her new name. Never say, "No, your name is _____," if your daughter uses her given name. Self-image, self-esteem and personal identity are closely tied to a person's name, and you don't want to create the perception of a good name/bad name.

We chose initially not to keep our daughter's given name but changed it to one that was similar, my grandmother's name, which we used as a middle name. Callie, who was three and a half at the time, adjusted to her new name quite well—or so we thought. It was only after about six months that I discovered the reason she wouldn't tell anyone her name. It was not because she didn't understand the question, as I had thought. She was unsure of how to answer because she knew what everyone called her and she answered to something different than what her name was. She was afraid to give the wrong answer. It was only after she was encouraged to answer with her given name that she started answering the question.

She then progressed to using both her new and given names. Learning about names and name recognition in pre-school helped her put first, middle, and last names in perspective. We still use her given name. It makes a great nickname because it means love. Because she was so attached to it, we added her given name back to her legal name when we finalized her re-adoption. If you find that you want to change your child's name, you can always do it at a later date.

Chapter 3

Baby Showers and Gift Registries

Showers for Adopted Children

There seems to be some confusion about whether it is appropriate to throw a shower for an adopted child. Let me set the record straight: It is a perfectly acceptable practice to throw a shower for an adopted child. While pregnancy is an exciting time for a mother-to-be, it is equally exciting or perhaps even more so for adoptive parents. First time parents may have undergone years of watching their friends and coworkers announce their pregnancies and suffering through or avoiding multiple baby showers. When it's finally their turn, no one deserves it more.

The hardest part of planning a shower for adoptive parents is trying to choose the date. In the case of international adoption, there can be unexpected delays and there is the outside chance that an adoption could fall through before or after the shower has been given. Even considering these unique situations, there are many creative ways to throw a shower for adoptive parents.

Types of Showers

A Secret Shower: This shower is perfect for people who receive permission to travel sooner than anticipated. Often these families have done little or no preparation and may need everything. A friend told me that this happened to a couple at her church. The women at her church bought much-needed baby items and wrapped them without cards and names. The items were delivered to the couple's home from the church, leaving them free to write one thank-you note rather than individual notes. This was a thoughtful option for a couple who had their hands full rearranging their household and adjusting to a new addition with short notice.

A One-Month or Coming-Out Shower: This shower is thrown a few weeks or a month after the child arrives. It's a great way to introduce friends to the new addition, and it gives both parents and child an adjustment period. This shower is ideal for toddlers and older children. After a few weeks, there is a good chance that the parents will have most of the essentials. Shopping is easy because guests know the sex and size of the child. Clothing is a good idea, as parents may not have purchased much in advance because size information may have been unavailable, and weight and height information may not be accurate. For infants, I like to buy clothes they can grow into. Photo albums, memory books and boxes, and picture frames become cherished keepsakes. Books are a great gift; and I also like to give educational videos, savings bonds, and, of course, toys.

The Traditional Shower: Although this type of shower can actually be the most helpful in preparing for a new child, it can also be the trickiest as they may require short notice. Friends or coworkers can tentatively plan showers and wait until a family receives a referral or travel approval to send out invitations.

Gift Registry

Gift registries for adopted children are an acceptable practice; in fact, it is easier for friends and family to make selections because older infants and toddlers have different needs and many traditional baby gifts are not appropriate. Appropriate gifts also depend on the child's developmental level, which in the case of internationally adopted children may be slightly delayed. I don't recommend registering for clothing because it is difficult to figure out the sizes until you actually see your child.

Retailers Don't Recognize Adoptive Families

Warning, warning! Be prepared for registry questionnaires that are not necessarily appropriate for an adopted child. I felt as though I had to constantly explain myself. It is also not uncommon to get strange looks from people who can't understand why you are doing a baby registry, talking about the shower you just had, or exchanging gifts when you don't look even slightly pregnant. One salesperson actually asked me if my purchase was for my first grandchild, which would be impossible unless I had had a child in my teens. Trust me, I didn't look that old!

I could not find any registry programs for adopted children, although there are many for parents of newborns and multiples. In fact, a representative from the largest toy and baby store on the East Coast sent me a handwritten note congratulating me on my pregnancy. They followed up with a customer service survey form. I informed them that while I appreciated a handwritten note, I was not pregnant—and the registrar knew that when I registered.

I also could not redeem their certificate for a diaper bag, since I would not be having a newborn and suggested they consider a registry program appropriate for adoptive parents. Though my friends spent hundreds of dollars in this store, the store representatives didn't bother to send me a reply. That was a valuable lesson. Now I save all correspondence I send to companies suggesting services for adopting parents and their children.

Request Services

As an adoptive parent with almost twenty years' retail experience, I urge everyone to contact the retailers whose stores they frequent and the manufacturers whose products they buy and request programs and services for adopted children. Until enough interest is expressed to show a growing market of adoptive parents, we will continue to be either excluded from or ineligible for many programs for new families.

Retailers are always looking for niche markets and trying to increase their market share. Recently, several companies have started to recognize adoptive families and include them in their advertising. Now is the time for adoptive families to flex their collective muscle. As in *Horton Hears a Who*, we need to keep saying, "We're here, we're here!"

Manufacturers use consumer requests in considering product/program development. As the number of adoptive families continues to increase, so does our importance as a consumer market. Your voice can make a difference. I say, ask, ask often, and ask loudly.

I send the following request to companies that I feel are missing programs that suit the needs of adoptive parents:

While you have programs for newborns and multiples, I noticed that you do not currently have any programs for adoptive parents/children. As a consumer who regularly uses your products, I would urge you to consider a program for adoptive families. Most internationally adopted babies are 6 to 24 months of age, not newborns. Adoptive families miss out on many special programs, promotional items, giveaways, etc., because there are no programs for adopted children—only infants, newborns, and multiples.

I urge you to use this request as often as you see fit. Adopted babies or toddlers are just as special as biological children are. When enough people request these services, companies will realize the validity of our request.

Return/Exchange Policies

Know the return/exchange policy of the stores where you shop and register. Is there a time limit for exchanges? Keeping sales receipts will help make returns and exchanges easier to process.

Because we believed we would be traveling to get our daughter within a month of our baby showers, we opened our presents and put her things where they belonged. However, unexpected delays within the foreign government kept us from traveling as expected. As a result, Callie had outgrown many items, which could not be returned because we had opened them. Don't open any items that could possibly be outgrown or left unused until after you get your travel date or you return home with your child. Stores should let you exchange basic merchandise that is part of their everyday assortment.

Usually, fashion items and clothing can only be returned/exchanged during the current selling season. If the item gets marked down, you will only be credited for the markdown price without the receipt. Don't hold onto an item that you suspect you will not be able to use. It's better to get a merchandise credit than to be stuck with an item you cannot use. Your friends will understand if your child was not able to wear the outfit that they bought. If you're afraid you'll hurt someone's feelings, try to exchange the clothing for a larger size.

When returning and exchanging merchandise, sympathetic salespeople can be your greatest allies. Don't be afraid to tell people you are adopting a child and you're not sure of her size, so you need a bigger size or a merchandise credit, or that your travel plans have been postponed, so now you need to return or exchange things your child has outgrown. One store manager was gracious enough to let me exchange a coat several months after the time limit had expired. Of course, it didn't hurt that the new coat I bought was two sizes larger and three times as expensive as the one I returned. However, if I had been afraid to ask or had not explained our situation, I would have had to buy a new coat as well as keep one that was too small.

Chapter 4

While You Are Waiting

While you are waiting to complete the adoption of your daughter, there are many things that you can do to occupy your time. Staying active will—at least in theory—help the time pass more quickly.

Actually this is probably an adoption myth. We all know once you commit to a country and complete your dossier that you can't wait to get a referral and jump on the next plane to China. No amount of busywork can truly take away that longing. However, you should make the most out of the time you have now; you will not have that luxury when your new addition arrives.

Meet Other Adoptive Families

Meeting and talking with other adoptive families helps creates a connection with someone who has been or is experiencing the same things you are. Adoptive families are unique, and often nonadoptive friends and families have a hard time comprehending what you are going through.

Unexpected delays, changes in procedures, or availability of children can all effect the waiting process. Acknowledge disappointments and keep communications open. Depend on your adoption agency to keep you up to date or dispel chat-room rumors.

For international adoptions, it can be beneficial to network with families who have recently been to the country, province, city, or even the same orphanage. Of course, there is no such thing as a sure thing, but you can get a general idea about what to expect while you are there.

It is also a good idea to find out what your options are concerning accommodations, restaurants, places to see, and places to shop. We spoke to several people who had recently traveled to our daughter's region. Having this information was a lifesaver and our facilitators were impressed that I knew so much about their city, hotels, and restaurants.

Parenting Classes

Take a parenting class. First-time parents may be understandably nervous or have no idea how to care for a baby or toddler. Unfortunately, unless you live in a larger metropolitan area, the only child-care classes available may be for expectant pregnant parents and many expectant adoptive parents may not feel comfortable in that environment. The majority of the information covered in these classes involves childbirth, hospital stays, and procedures. I was relieved when we arrived to find that we were not the only adoptive couple there.

Another option is to take a child-care course for child-care providers. Check with your local Red Cross or technical colleges to see what type of classes they offer. In addition to child-care classes, you should take an infant or child CPR class.

One of the hospitals in our area has started offering classes for adoptive parents. They are for newborn/infant care and are by special request. If the classes you need are not available, try requesting that they add the type of program you need. A local hospital was very open to providing more adoption classes. Little did I know at the time, that I would be the one teaching them.

 ## Lifebooks

Start a lifebook. Lifebooks may be more appropriate for adopted children than tradtional baby books. It should include information from birth, to adoption, and beyond.

It is a great way to record special moments in a child's life. Include pictures of the child's birth country, your adoption journey, plane tickets, newspapers, hotel brochures, artwork, etc. A great resource is Lifebooks: *Creating a Treasure for the Adopted Child* by Beth O' Malley. Another is *Our Chosen Child: How You Came To Us And The Growing Up Years,* by Judy Pelikan and Judith Levy.

Preschool Programs

Check out your daycare and preschool options. Your needs will vary greatly depending on when and if you will be returning to work. Sign up for the waiting list if necessary. If an adoption will be completed shortly, you may have to begin making payments to ensure your child's space is held.

Our daughter was three-and-a-half years old at the time of her adoption. Her developmental level was more like that of a two-and-a-half- to three-year-old. We decided not to rush her into a preschool program. We formed an adoption playgroup. We had also joined a Mommies Day Out program for several months but found that it did not have enough structure. Check out similar programs and make sure that it is a structured learning environment. It may be counterproductive for one of your child's first classroom experiences to be one of chaos, including little supervised play, inconsistent caretakers, and little educational value.

Daycare and preschool programs should have an open-door policy and encourage parent participation. I inquired about observing one 4K class I had considered for Callie and was told no because it was considered disruptive to the classroom. The teacher went on to tell me that the policy was to protect the children's privacy and that they had parent open house once a year. I don't believe four-year-olds "right to privacy" is more important than a parent's right to observe a classroom when trying to choose a safe and appropriate school program. We did not apply to that program.

Learn the Language

If you are adopting internationally, learn some of the basics in your child's native language. At the very minimum, you should learn some basic greetings, polite phrases, and questions and answers. In addition you may also wish to learn numbers, terms of endearment, adoption terms, parenting terms, and things related to food and shopping. Your host will appreciate the effort, and it may be comforting to your child if you can say a few words or phrases that she can understand.

This is especially helpful if you are adopting a toddler or older child. The two primary dialects of Chinese are Mandarin and Cantonese. Mandarin is used for government business, and in the educational system. In Beijing most people speak Mandarin while in Guangzhou they speak Cantonese. The province that your daughter resides in should help determine whether she speaks Cantonese or Mandarin. This information may be included in the referral information that you receive.

Most bookstores have an assortment of foreign-language materials. Depending on what is available, you may have to special-order them. Available programs include *Berlitz Passport to 31 Languages, Berlitz Phrase Book and*

Dictionary (these are great to carry in a handbag or pocket), *Living Languages In-Flight Programs,* and Teresa Kellehers *Adopting from China, a Language and Parenting Guide.*

Other resources adoptive parents have found useful are Rosetta Stone Chinese, Chinese at a Glance, and Chinese 1, (Mandarin) Pimsleur Language Program.

Sending Gifts to China

If you would like to send a gift to your child's orphanage, foster parents or a camera to have pictures taken of your child, you may want to contact Adele's Services for Adoptive Parents of Chinese Children at www.blessedkids.com. This may include fresh cake, flowers, fruit baskets, a birthday package, or an item you wish to send such as a photo album for older children. In addition they can provide, documents translation (letters), translate child's name, and orphanage address's.

Rest and Relaxation

A stressed-out mommy can make for a stressed-out family. It is important to take care of yourself while you are preparing for your adoption. Infertility and grief alone can cause crisis-level stress. Add waiting or delays, and some days you might have to make yourself get out of bed. Sometimes it's good to play hooky and stay in bed all day.

If you look good, you'll feel good. Have your nails done; get a pedicure or a massage. Have a makeover, try a new haircut, or color your hair. Always wanted to be a blonde? Now's a great time to go for it!

Try wearing bright colors instead of muted or dark shades. Play dress-up; try on clothing in the latest styles or colors even if you think it's not for you—you might be surprised. Update your wardrobe and get rid of any baggy, pregnant-wannabe clothes. Have "glamour photos" taken, or make your own calendar. Some other things that can help are:

- Cook a favorite time-consuming meal instead of takeout
- Don't overextend yourself, especially during the holidays
- Go to quiet, dimly lit restaurants instead of loud, crowded bars and restaurants

- Have quiet, intimate evenings with a few friends instead of large parties
- If you host an annual event, see if a friend would be willing to host this year
- Listen to jazz or classical music
- Spend a day at a spa
- Take a relaxing bubble bath
- Take a small vacation
- Unplug the phone (This is a hard one if you are waiting for "the call.")
- Use candles at dinner
- Visit a favorite childhood spot

Diet and Exercise

Now is probably not the best time to start a diet. Caffeine, chocolate, and doughnuts are good antidotes to stress. My medicine of choice is sugar cookies with frosting and birthday cake.

If you do not have a daily exercise routine, now is a good time to start. When you travel to bring home your daughter, you may do a large amount of walking or be on your feet longer than usual. Carrying around or picking up a baby or toddler without having the opportunity to become accustomed to it can result in backache or injury. Walking twenty to thirty minutes a day can help increase your stamina and is good for your back.

If you skip the sodas, chocolate or doughnuts, you may even lose a few pounds. This could be an added bonus, especially if you are carrying around twenty-five or thirty pounds of IVF/fertility-drug-induced "side effects."

Chinese Food

While you are in China you will have the opportunity to sample real Chinese food rather than the Americanized version. If you are not familiar with Chinese food, now is a good time to start. Begin with learning the different types and styles.

Once you have decided which is best suited for your taste, experiment and practice cooking Chinese. (Dialing for take out does not count). And finally, learn to use chopsticks.

Read

Now is the time to study up. Read parenting, toddler, and adoption books. Read travel books, guides or maps. Read up on places you will visit or read current books on China. Consider subscribing to China Today Magazine, China Tourism Magazine or reading other books and periodicals available at www.chinabooks.com.

Reading is also a great way to take your mind off your adoption. Read for leisure, study up on a hobby or sport, read the biography of someone you admire, or read trashy romance novels! Reread an old favorite, finish the one you already started but haven't had time to finish, or read something you've always wanted to read.

Paperwork

You thought you were through with the paperwork. Now is a good time to gather the documents needed for your child's Social Security card. Find out what is needed to obtain your child's passport, the requirements for re-adoption, state subsidies or grants, or tax information. Complete any paperwork that you can in advance, including insurance and medical forms.

Make Name Cards

In China it is a common practice to exchange name cards (business cards). You should either take your business cards, or make some which may simply include you and your spouses name, address, and phone number.

Exchanging name cards has its own special protocol. The proper way to give someone your business card is to hold it with two hands, one on each corner, so that the recipient can read it. When you are given a name card, you should appear to study it briefly and then comment on how impressed you are with their card.

Keeping Busy

Nothing makes me feel better than shopping. Shop for your new arrival, and make the purchases necessary to begin life as a family. Complete a gift registry, purchase gifts and donations for your trip, or do your Christmas shopping early. The following will also help keep you busy: You didn't know you had so much work to do did you?

- Childproof your house
- Clean the house
- Complete your nursery
- Develop an orphanage project/donation collection
- Finish a project
- Get immunizations
- Have the carpets cleaned
- Have the house painted
- Keep a diary
- Learn about children's toys
- Learn to change a diaper
- Make a list of questions to ask your child's caregiver
- Pick adoption announcements
- Plan the christening
- Plant flowers, bulbs, or gardens
- Purchase items you will need for your trip
- Purchase orphanage gifts
- Renovate/redecorate your bathroom
- Rent and watch movies about China
- Research children's services
- Select a pediatrician
- Select godparents
- Stock your pantry
- Write your will

Chapter 5

The Wardrobe

Shopping for Your New Arrival

The first thing I did after we accepted the referral of our daughter was buy a pair of toddler bunny slippers. (In my defense, it was May and they were on sale.) Three dresses, a short set, and a package of socks followed the slippers. I was afraid if I didn't buy ahead that there would be nothing to choose from when it was time to travel. With a little help from my mother, by the time we were supposed to travel to Russia, I had a complete summer wardrobe for a thirteen-month-old child.

I found that planning and updating a wardrobe for our daughter was on some levels therapeutic. (I love being able to justify shopping.) At the time of our adoption, our nursery had been completed for about a year and shopping for clothing was one way I could continue to plan for the arrival of our child. While there are some things she had outgrown and could not use, it was still cheaper than therapy would have been!

What Size Clothing?

Generally speaking, if you are adopting a child in the United Sates, you would probably be given accurate clothing and shoe sizes. Those who adopt internationally may not have that luxury and children adopted from China are usually smaller than their peers in the United States. Adoptive families must depend on orphanage directors, facilitators, or adoption agencies to provide the most up-to-date, accurate information available. Families frequently are given correct measurements including height, weight, but leg length, foot length, and arm length is information that you are less likely to receive.

When we began procedures for adopting Callie, we requested current size and weight information. Her records had not been updated in almost a year. Because there was such a difference in size, we believed one or both of the size reports were inaccurate. Our daughter's "updated" measurements, taken six months before her adoption, were still five pounds light. She was so small that the doctor at the U.S. embassy weighed her twice because he thought something was wrong with the scales. When we factored in how much we thought she should have grown, we ended up taking size 3T and 4T clothing. Callie was really a 2T, but most of the outfits fit by the following spring. You can purchase clothing that is the correct size when you return home.

For a growth charts for Chinese chidlren see http://www.fwcc.org/growthchart.html at Families with Children from China.

What Size Shoes?

One question that perplexed me for days was "What size shoes will she wear?" Although our figures were inaccurate, we were able to estimate clothing size but we had no way to get any information about shoe size. After consulting with both children's apparel and shoe buyers, the answer was quite simple: There is no way to know what size shoes you will need. You will have to estimate based on age and size and have several different-size pairs on hand.

You may need to measure your daughter's feet to see what size shoes she will wear. To do this, trace her foot on a piece of paper. Take this measurement with or without socks, depending on if they will be worn with the shoes. Measure the longest part of the foot from the longest toe to the heel. Use the following infant and toddler size chart for conversion.

Shoe Size	Foot Length in Inches
1	$3^8/_{16}$
2	$3^7/_8$
3	$4^3/_{16}$
4	$4^1/_2$
5	$4^{13}/_{16}$
6	$5^1/_8$
7	$5^1/_2$
8	$5^3/_4$

For young baby's booties, or slippers with suede, padded bottoms can be bought in China. If you plan on taking baby shoes, take one pair of inexpensive white or black shoes that can be left in China, or sent to the orphanage if they don't fit.

Most of the shoes Callie wore during our orphanage visits did not fit. Her little feet stuck out of the sides of her sandals. They were also so well worn they would not have been sold at a resale shop. If you take shoes as an orphanage donation, leather or leather-look shoes can be cleaned more easily and will last longer than canvas shoes.

Whoever invented shoes with Velcro closures was a genius. Kids can put them on or take them off by themselves. I really liked this aspect of the shoes that I left at the orphanage. I had seen the children slip buckled shoes on and off.

Clothing Sizes and Size Charts

Between the time I managed a children's clothing store and the time we started the adoption process, the sizes for children's clothing were changed. Now in addition to the standard sizes of 18 months, 24 months, 2T, and so on, we now have sizes like infant, XX-small, and 3 years. Somewhere along the way, the new "in" stores decided to create their own sizes. Thankfully the manufacturers that have been in the business for years did not change standard industry sizing.

Basically this inconsistency in children's clothing sizes requires you to know multiple size charts depending on the store. In essence, if you shop at a department store or a discount store, your child will wear one size (with the exception of a few designer brands that may be available), but if you shop at Baby Gap or Old Navy, for example, your child will wear multiple sizes.

I stumbled on this phenomenon quite by accident when a friend, whose child was much younger than the one we were adopting, asked me what size our child was and then replied that her son wore the same size. I knew that, with the age difference, this could not possibly be true. I can't imagine the confusion that this has caused gift-givers all over the country. I had firsthand experience with this problem when I was given the size for my cousin's daughter, 24 months. Was this 24 months the size that should fit a 25- to 28-pound child or the size that should fit a two-year-old? Adding to the confusion was the fact that she was only eighteen months old.

The following size charts are two examples of how children's clothing sizes may vary:

Size	Weight (pounds)	Height (inches)
0–5 months	7–13	Up to 24
6–9 months	14–19	24–28
12 months	20–22	28–30
18 months	23–25	31–32
24 months	26–28	33–35
2T	26–28	33–35
3T	29–33	36–38
4T	34–38	39–41

Size	Age	Height (inches)	Weight (pounds)
Newborn	3–6 months	21–23	12–17
Infant	6–12 months	24–28	18–22
XX–Small	12–18 months	28–31	22–27
X–Small	18 months–2 years	32–34	28–32
Small	2–3 years	35–38	32–35
Medium	3–4 yrs.	39–42	35–41 lbs.
Large	4–5 yrs.	42–46	41–50 lbs.

Metric Measures and Equivalents

Since most measurements that you receive from international adoptions are in metric increments, you will need a conversion chart. I included this one because I have had to refer to it several times.

Length

1 millimeter (mm)		= 0.0394 in.
1 centimeter (cm)	= 10 mm	= 0.3937 in.
1 meter (m)	= 1000 mm	= 1.0936 yd
1 kilometer (km)	= 1000 m	= 0.6214 mi.

Weight

1 milligram (mg)		= 0.0154 grain
1 gram (g)	= 1000 mg	= 0.0353 oz.
1 kilogram (kg)	= 1000 g	= 2.2046 lbs.
1 tonne (t)	= 1000 kg	= 1.1023 short tons or = 0.9842 long ton

Area

1 sq. centimeter (cm. sq.)	= 100 mm sq.	= 0.155 sq. in.
1 sq. meter (m sq.)	= 10,000 cm sq.	= 1.1196 sq. yd
1 hectare (ha)	= 10,000 m sq.	= 2.4711 acres
1 sq. kilometer (km sq.)	= 100 ha	= 0.3861 sq. mi.

Volume

1 cubic centimeter (cm^3)		= 0.061 in^3
1 cubic decimeter (dm^3)	= 1000 cm^3	= 0.0353 ft^3
1 cubic meter (m^3)	= 1000dm^3	= 1.3079 yd^3
1 liter (L)	= 1 dm^3	= 0.2642 gal
1 hectoliter (hL)	= 0 100 L	= 2.8378 bu

Temperature

Celsius = 5/9 (F-32 degrees)

Fahrenheit = 9/5 (C+32 degrees)

Celsius	-25	-18	-10	0	10	20	30	40
Fahrenheit	-13	0	14	32	50	68	86	104

Climate and Culture

Once you have a rough estimate of what size your daughter will wear, you will have to determine what her needs are. One of the largest factors affecting your daughter's clothing needs is what time of year you will be traveling to China. You also need to consider weather, climate, season, and accuracy of available size information, cultural requirements, and the child's age.

You may or may not be able to keep the clothes that your daughter is wearing when you receive custody of her. This will depend upon the orphanage and whether your child is in foster care. Ask ahead of time what the procedure is and if you are allowed to keep her in the clothes she is wearing. If so, do not be in a hurry to change her clothes. Sometimes handoff from Nanny to new Mommy is fast and can be traumatic. Waiting to change her clothes may help reduce this. Make sure to bring replacements clothes to give to give in exchange for the clothes you are keeping.

If your daughter leaves the orphanage wearing the clothes that you bring for her, you will probably want this to be a special outfit; it will be the one you have the first pictures taken in, pictures that you'll cherish forever. You will want to make sure that this outfit and the rest of the clothing that you bring for your child are seasonally appropriate and are in accordance with the customs of your host country. These customs could include wearing hats, not wearing shorts, or always wearing long sleeves. Remember that your child's caregivers will be observing you, and they want to make sure you are dressing her appropriately.

Easy-Access Clothing

When possible, you may want to avoid clothing that has lots of buckles, buttons, snaps, or zippers. As a new parent, this will only add to your frustration when you are trying to learn to dress a moving target or undress one quickly. I like to avoid "onsies" and other one-piece clothing with snaps, especially for toddlers who are at least partially potty trained. Remember: you want easy-access, no-fuss clothing.

When we adopted our daughter from Russia, we had custody of her for less than forty-eight hours when we returned to the United States. During the first leg of our trip, which included a ninety-minute flight to Moscow and a quick stop at a photographer's office before her embassy visit, she wore three dresses and two or three diapers.

Trying to get a sick toddler, whom we'd only had custody of for twelve hours, into an airplane bathroom to change her dirty diaper and clothing was quite an enlightening experience. New foods and new sensations helped contribute to her upset stomach, vomiting, and diarrhea.

To help determine how much clothing you will need, you need to take into consideration how long you will be in China with your child and what laundry options are available. Fortunately, we had same-day service for laundry at the hotels where we stayed.

The Basic Wardrobe

You will probably need to take a minimum of six outfits for your child. I recommend taking two outfits that should fit according to the estimated size information, two to three outfits that are the next size up, and maybe one that is a size smaller. You will probably want to take clothing that can be layered or mixed and matched. Consider the following clothing options:

- Arrive home outfit
- Boots and galoshes
- Coat or snowsuit
- Dresses, jumpers
- Hair bows/barrettes
- Hats, scarves, gloves/mittens
- Jacket/Sweater Jeans or pants
- Pants/short sets
- Pajama's or gown
- Rain poncho/rain coat
- Shoes, socks or tights
- Sun hat
- Sweaters
- Swimsuit
- T-shirts, undershirts
- Turtlenecks, shirts, blouses
- Underwear/disposable training pants or diapers

Until you actually see your child in person, you probably will not want to purchase a large amount of clothing. To save on expenses, buy clothing from consignment shops, accept hand-me-downs, and borrow clothes from friends. Once you're home, fill in the wardrobe gaps. Don't over purchase—most likely your child will have a growth surge her first year home.

The following guideline will help you plan for your babies clothing needs:

Late Spring, Summer, and Early Fall

1-2 hats/caps (required)

1 sweater or jacket

7 onsies (to wear in room, are climate friendly and wash and dry easily)

2-3 other outfits (to wear out)

2-3 Dresses

1-2 warmer outfits (for cooler conditions)

1 warm blanket

2-3 receiving blankets

4-6 pairs of socks

1 pair of shoes (buy a second one there)

Late Fall, Winter and Early Spring

2 hats

1-2 sweaters or jackets

1 winter coat (coat/bunting should cover legs for children under the age of one)

1 pair of gloves/mittens

4 onsies (to wear underclothing)

5-7 or more warm outfits

2 warm blankets

2 receiving blankets

1 pair of shoes (buy a second one there)

6 pairs of socks

Miscellaneous

cloth diapers (2)

diaper covers

hairbows

hooded towel

pacifier w/leash

washcloths (4)

This simple outline helps provide the minimum basics you would need for toddlers or older children until you return home. Interchange summer and winter items as necessary.

Girl's Basic Wardrobe

1 special outfit

2 dress's

1 jumper and blouse

3 pants sets

2 or 3 turtlenecks or knit tops

1 pair of casual shoes

6 pairs of socks or tights

6 pairs of underwear/undershirts

1 sweater, cardigan, or jacket

1 hat

Boy's Basic Wardrobe

3 pants sets

2 pairs of jeans or khaki pants

6 knit shirts or turtlenecks

1 pair sneakers or casual shoes

6 pairs of socks

6 pairs of underwear/undershirts

1 sweater or jacket

1 hat or cap

Chapter 6

The Nursery

I believe the process of planning a nursery is similar to that of planning a wedding. For years you've dreamed about it—picked colors, picked a theme, and imagined the big day when you bring your child home. Planning your future with your daughter is no different than planning a future with your spouse, make the most of it and enjoy this wonderfully frantic time.

The first thing I did was to decide which colors I would use in the nursery. After spending hours and eventually taking my husband on a shopping excursion (I was getting desperate), we finally decided on a comforter set that ultimately determined the color as well as the theme for the nursery: multicolored pastels with moons and stars. After you decide what colors and theme you want for your nursery, you are ready for the essentials.

Nursery Essentials

When choosing furniture (the crib, dresser, changing table, rocking chair, etc.), think ahead. Ask yourself if it's something you can use for a second child, if the color is neutral, if it's convertible, if it can be used in a different room later. The crib we chose converts from a toddler to a full-size bed, and the changing table is a short dresser fitted with a changing pad. When your child outgrows a changing table or you find that you don't use it, simply remove the changing pad.

Callie's bedroom set is a neutral light pine. A white bedroom set would have been beautiful in our nursery, but it wouldn't have been practical to use for a boy. You may also want to choose neutral colors for the nursery, especially for items that can be used again such as the changing pad, sheets, and blankets

Here is a list of essential items for your nursery:

- Baby-size pillow
- Bed rail (if using a regular bed instead of a crib)
- Blankets
- Changing table
- Changing table pad
- Comforter set
- Crib bumper pad
- Crib or bed
- Diaper stacker
- Dresser
- Mattress
- Rocking chair
- Sheets

The Crib

The crib mattress should be firm and should fit the crib snugly so that no more than two fingers fit between the mattress and the crib. A firm mattress will help keep the crib sheets in place, too. Crib slats should not be more than two inches apart. If your child starts out in a daybed rather than a crib, you may want to use a bed rail to help prevent falls.

Most infant comforter sets include one set of sheets, a comforter, a bumper pad, and a diaper stacker. I consider a diaper stacker optional and probably would not have bought one had it not been included in my set. Crib bumpers should not be used once a toddler can pull herself up on top of them, because they can be used as steps to climb out of the crib. Baby pillows are optional depending on the age and developmental level of your child and should be used with discretion. You may want to buy individual bedding pieces rather than buying a comforter set. Depending on your daughter's age, you may not be able to use all the components of a set.

When I registered for my baby shower, I requested one set of sheets in addition to those that came in the comforter set. It wasn't until later that I looked at a baby registry checklist and saw their recommendation of at least three or four sets of sheets. I picked four baby blankets in different fabrics and weights.

I also picked an additional blanket in a light jersey knit that could be packed in a diaper bag or played with. We take it everywhere.

A Crib or a Bed?

If you are adopting an older infant or toddler, you will not use a crib for the usual length of time, from infancy through the transition to a toddler or larger bed, I think the smart choice is a bed that can convert from a crib to a toddler bed. The bed I chose converts from a crib to a toddler bed and then to a full-size bed. Choose a bed that can convert to two different mattress heights when used as a crib. For a toddler, the bed would probably be used at the lowest setting; you many never need the upper setting.

In our case, we started the adoption process to adopt a fifteen-month-old toddler and ended up with a three-year-old. For our daughter, we skipped the crib stage and went straight to the toddler daybed. For future children, infant or young toddler, we will be able to use the crib setting. A crib would have only been usable for another infant. Our daughter slept in a regular bed at the time of the adoption. It was not as big or as tall as a twin bed. It was a more like a modified toddler bed with no side rails. At 34 inches and 26½ pounds, she was technically small enough to fit in a crib, but she could have easily climbed out. She also grew 6 inches within the first year home.

The philosophy of when to move a toddler from a crib is subjective. Some people say when your child is 35 inches tall, she should be moved to a toddler or regular-size bed. Others say at thirty months of age or when the toddler starts climbing out of the crib. To be safe, check manufacturer's guidelines when purchasing the bed. Although some toddlers are probably large enough to skip the crib and go straight to a toddler or regular-size bed, many internationally adopted children are small for their age and are developmentally delayed.

I liked the idea of having the extra protection of a crib as a "containment field" while we adjusted to having a mobile toddler in the house while we were asleep. Crib extenders can be purchased if the crib's sides are not high enough.

Sleeping Arrangements

If possible, try to find out what type of bed your child is sleeping in now and what her sleeping arrangements are. Sleeping customs vary by culture. Children adopted from orphanages may have never slept in a room by themselves, may be used to sleeping in daylight, and with constant noise.

Most babies adopted from Chinese orphanages sleep in cribs. Children in foster care probably sleep in the same bed as their foster parents. This would probably be a wood frame bed with a bamboo mat. Children adopted from other Asian countries may have similar sleeping practices as in China or sleep on a mattress on the floor or in hammocks.

Find out as much information about sleeping arrangements as you can. This will help you plan ahead for disruptive sleep patterns and ease any sleep discomfort or distress.

Babies who are not used to sleeping in a quiet room may be soothed to sleep with the aid of a white noise machine.

Babies who have spent a large amount of time in a crib may have thin or balding hair on the back of their heads. Healthy infants and young or small toddlers should be placed on their backs to sleep. This will reduce the risk of Sudden Infant Death Syndrome (SIDS).

Overseas travel can result in jet lag. A newly arrived toddler may not be adjusted to the difference in time zones and may want to sleep all day and "party all night." She may have to be eased into sleeping in a crib, sleeping by herself, or sleeping in a dark or quiet room. You will probably learn by trial and error. Be prepared to have new arrivals sleep with you at least for the first few nights you are home.

Stressful Sleep

For most children things that are scary, tend to be even more so at night. You may notice that initially your daughter may be afraid to go to sleep. She may even cry when she is asleep. If your child is in obvious distress over bedtime, try to identify any objects that she may think are scary. Because children in orphanages have the least amount of adult interaction when they are put to bed, their can be a lot of things seemingly harmless items that become scary to them, it could be curtains, curtains blowing from an open window, a door open (or closed) or even toys or pictures that are different than they are accustomed to; cartoon characters versus real people or animals.

Being overtired or under stress can cause night terrors. Most all children have an occasional night terror and they are different for each child. During a night terror a child will cry, and possibly be inconsolable. They may or may not have their eyes open, they appear awake but they actually are not. While this can be scary for parents, children usually go back to sleep, and rarely have any memory of the event. The best course of action is not to try to wake them but soothe them instead by speaking softly, rubbing their back, etc.

It is not uncommon for children who are adopted from orphanages to rock. Rocking which is a form of self-stimulation and comforting behavior is seen most often when a child is under duress, tired, or when they are in new circumstances. Some children rock when they do not want to go to sleep while other can not sleep without rocking. themselves to sleep. Rocking can be attributed to the fact that no one rocked your child when she needed it so she learned to do it herself. Rocking may be accompanied by thumb sucking and moving the fingers in front of the face.

Depending on how hard a child rocks it can be very scary looking. Imagine the way your fingers are rolled from one side to the other when you went to the USCIS office to have your fingerprints done. Even as an experienced adoptive parent, I was unnerved the first time I saw my son rock. The best thing to do is to pick your daughter up and rock her, snuggle with her or rub her back: anything that will synchronize rhythm as opposed to her solitary movement. Most children grow out of rocking. As thier comfort level increases, you should see a decrease in your child's need to rock.

Often parents of toddlers who have problems sleeping at night are told to let them cry it out. This technique is not appropriate for adopted children who are insecurely attached. Allowing an adopted child who is not securely attached to her parents to cry it out can impede the attachment process.

Wall and Window Treatments

Wall and window treatments in the nursery may include the following:

- Blinds or shades
- Lamp(s)
- Nightlight
- Pictures
- Wall hangings
- Window treatments

Your daughter probably has the least amount of supervision while she is in the bed. Check the crib's placement in the nursery. Make sure that she can't reach wall hangings, pictures, or mirrors. A toddler can pull down pictures and mirrors on top of herself and get caught or tangled in wall hangings. Furniture placement is also important because a toddler can use other pieces of furniture to climb out of the crib. Check the outside area around the crib; you don't want your daughter to land on anything that could hurt her once she figures out how to escape from the crib.

While our daughter has always slept through the night, she would not get out of her bed without permission because of her orphanage training. She had been home over a year before she understood that it was okay to get up in the morning or if she needed to go to the bathroom. Her friend Viktoria, who was adopted at two-and-a-half years old, was just the opposite. Her mother frequently found that she had been out of the bed or was out of the bed when she checked on her. All toys, books, and the chest of drawers were fair game when Vika was out of bed. Make sure any toys with small parts and baby products are out of reach.

Blinds and shades should be lead-free. If your blinds are old, they may not be lead-free, and the dust buildup on them could include lead particles. A cord wind-up should be used on blinds to prevent the possibility of accidents involving tangled cords. Mobiles should not be used on toddler cribs; however, there are some crib toys that you may be able to use if you wish. Check the manufacturer's recommendation; this should tell you if it would be safe for a toddler to use them.

Lamps and nightlights should be out of a child's reach because both are burn hazards. Use cord roll-ups for lamps and other items with electrical cords to prevent toddlers from pulling these items off on top of them by the cord.

Miscellaneous

- Baby monitor
- Chew guard
- Clothes hangers and hamper
- Humidifier/vaporizer
- Lifebooks, Memory box
- Pacifier
- Picture frames and album
- Pillow pal
- Small laundry bag
- Snugglies
- Teething ring

Consider the layout of your house. You may need a baby monitc nursery if your house is two stories, if the bedrooms are not close together, or if the bedrooms are removed from the main living space. Each child is different and some will need more supervision than others will when they are alone in their rooms.

Your new daughter may not need a pacifier, but she may still be cutting teeth. A teething ring can help soothe sore teeth and gums. A chew guard will help protect your daughter's teeth as well as prevent damage to the crib.

You may need hangers for your daughter's clothing. I bought a small mesh laundry bag, made for small delicate items, to put our daughter's socks and tights in while they were in the washing machine. Her socks were so small I was afraid I would never find all the mates after I did laundry.

Picture frames, lifebooks, memory boxes, and picture albums will become treasured keepsakes. At the time, I couldn't find a baby book that I thought was appropriate for our daughter. I chose a regular picture album, which also had two coordinating memory boxes and a video cover. I used the larger memory box for regular keepsakes and mementos. The smaller memory box I put aside for the special keepsakes that I want Callie to have when she is grown. The video cover is for the video of the first time we met her.

We have a small photo album that we used for photos of our trip. I wanted to be able to show our photos without them being mishandled. It is what I consider our "baby's first pictures." The album includes pictures of the three of us at the orphanage, sightseeing, and when we first arrived home. It is a treasured diary of our trip.

Pillow pals are animal-shaped pillows that can be used to play with or lie on in the crib or on the floor while watching TV. I like to think of them as functional stuffed animals that can be washed. (Check the manufacturer's label.) At night I sat our daughter's pillow pal in the floor next to her bed to help cushion her fall if she managed to get out of the crib. Snugglies, like Pillow Buddies, can be used to help soothe toddlers; they are stuffed animals with a blanket body. A Snugglie eliminates the need for two separate items to search for.

After watching her cousin Kelsey with a treasured "baby," someone gave Callie one that was similar. She became instantly attached to this little pink bear and has slept with it at naptime and every night since. Losing this bear would be traumatic. I recommend purchasing an emergency backup for any well-loved "baby."

A humidifier or vaporizer is helpful for relieving stuffy noses caused by dry air. If you have central heat, you will probably want to invest in one to help prevent sleeplessness and wakeful toddlers.

Chapter 7

The Toy Box

No household would be complete without a wide assortment of toys, and your daughter will spend many happy hours playing with them. Choose toys that are appropriate for your daughter's developmental age rather than those for her chronological age. For example: toys for children over three may not be appropriate for newly adopted three-year-olds. They may not know not to put small parts in their mouths, and these toys may be too complex for them to play with as intended.

Your daughter may have little experience with toys or may have only been allowed to play with a few. Do not be surprised if you have to show her how to play with many of the toys that you have. Too many toys or a room full of toys may be overwhelming for a newly adopted child. Start slowly and follow her lead.

Beginning Basics

Blocks, balls, and container toys are great first toys for children. They stimulate children to reach for them and help teach manipulation, spatial relations, and hand-and-eye coordination. Toys should stimulate mental association, play familiar tunes, and help teach object permanence. Your daughter will enjoy stacking, throwing, and putting things in and dumping them out of containers.

Children are drawn to light and sound and any toys that have buttons, bells, or whistles. Most will enjoy anything that plays music. Musical instruments such as pianos, xylophones, drums, or tambourines will provide your daughter with hours of fun.

Hide-and-seek, peak-a-boo, and patty-cake are favorite games. As your daughter becomes more mobile, push/pull toys such as cars, doll strollers, shopping carts, cars or animals with a pull cord, mini cars, lawnmowers, or other toys that imitate familiar everyday activities will be favorites.

Toys for Older Toddlers

Older toddlers will acquire new skills such as matching or sorting objects by size and color, recognizing numbers and letters, and fine motor skills. Puzzles, memory matching games, videos, books, and refrigerator magnets with ABCs and numbers are fun and educational.

Ring-around-the-rosy, itsy-bitsy spider, and "the wheels on the bus" will become familiar favorites. Children learn by imitation and will want to mimic the activities of others. They will want to cook, serve food, drive, clean house, or feed their babies.

As older toddlers become more mobile, you will have to take more precautions in your home. Flowerpots might become sandboxes and toilets might be used as a bathtub for a doll. While getting ready to attend a citizenship party for adopted children hosted by our congressional representative, Jim DeMint, I finished applying my makeup only to look down and find Callie had applied her own lipstick. At least she picked red, which coordinated with her dress. Anything within a toddler's reach is fair game and you will find that they are quite ingenious.

Baby Dolls and Snuggly Toys

Except for rare occasions, Callie did not want to sleep with any of her dolls or stuffed animals in the bed. That all changed when she met Baby Bear, a little pink stuffed bear that is actually a baby toy with a rattle inside. Since she received her "baby," she has become very attached to it and has not slept a single night without it. Because she is so attached, I found a backup in case something ever happened to her beloved little bear.

I like stuffed animals that are soft and fluffy. These are great for kids to snuggle with, and I especially like ones that can be washed. I do not care for many of the ones that sing or dance and need batteries. They are not soft; they are not washable and are not particularly toddler-proof.

One of Callie's favorite dolls was Zoë, which had clothes that buttoned, snapped, and tied. Another is her *kookla* ("doll" in Russian), which was the closest thing to handmade that I could find. This was the doll that we gave her when she left the orphanage. Callie also had a lifesize doll that had red hair the same color as a friend at school. She liked to carry her around the house.

Any type of doll brings out the maternal instinct in Callie. She will rock, sing to, feed, and drive them in their stroller. Thanks to Gramma, she has the deluxe baby stroller complete with baby carrier. Of course, she also has baby clothes, bottles, and brushes. She has lots of dishes, and her babies are well fed. She is quite the hostess and frequently serves tea from her tiny silver tea set that her Aunt Merry gave her.

Using Toys for Teaching

If your child will be in a new environment or, as in our daughter's case, requires hospitalization and surgery, toys can help prepare them by familiarizing them with the objects or location in which they will be exposed. Before Callie had surgery, we purchased the *Sesame Street Visits the Hospital* video. We also bought a medical kit. It is still a favorite toy for the future "Dr. Hoppenhauer," who really likes to give people shots. Because Callie would be required to wear arm splints for at least a week after her cleft palate surgery, we played hospital with a stuffed bear. At the advice of Alex's mom, who had done the same thing for him, Mr. Bear had to wear bandages and arm splints. He also had his temperature taken, his mouth and ears checked, his heart and lungs listened to, his blood pressure taken, and more. This type of play can help children feel more comfortable in new situations—especially a place as scary as the hospital.

Teaching with toys or role-playing with them can put a child at ease and help her have a better understanding of a situation, even if she can't fully appreciate what is happening or if there is a language barrier.

Children's Books

I can't say enough about books. Books are one of my favorite gifts for children. I believe that storybooks and reading to your children, as well as books that teach, help set the foundation for further education and learning. They also help increase vocabulary, improve reading comprehension, and instill a desire and the ability to continue to learn.

While your child is learning English, reading to her will help her learn the language. One book that I bought for our daughter was the *Fisher-Price Wordbook*. It contained more than 500 words, complete with illustrations. I thought the pictures would help keep Callie entertained while she got a lesson in English. Although this book was probably meant for toddlers, I believe it could also be used for children up to six years of age.

One of my all-time favorite children's books is Dr. Seuss's *The Cat in the Hat Beginner Book Dictionary*. This book has examples of words that begin with each letter of the alphabet. Each word is illustrated and accompanied by a sentence that uses the word. I can't tell you how many times I referred to this dictionary when I wanted to draw something that was illustrated in it. No child should be without this book.

Books that involve naming or moving body parts, numbers, or colors will help keep your active toddler occupied while teaching them new words. In my effort to keep our daughter bilingual, I learned all the names of the body parts in Russian and read them to her in both Russian and English.

You can find a variety of books that take place in or are about China, and adoption from China. Some of these may have to be specially ordered from adoption-related Web sites. www.Asiaforkids.com is a great resource. China for Children Magazine can be ordered at www.ocdf.org/magazine

Educational Toys, Videos, Tapes, and CDs

When we adopt a child, we often find that we adopt our child's country and culture. World history has always been of interest, and I find that multiculturalism is now a favorite subject. There are a variety of language and educational materials available for children that help promote this multiculturalism.

Sesame Street—Big Bird in China is a great place to start. This CD is available from Sony Music or at Amazon.com, ASIN B00016XO6U.

Teach Me tapes are children's cassettes that are available in many different languages. Some teach words or phrases while others contain songs or nursery rhymes. When we purchased the *Teach Me Russian* cassette, (also available in Chinese) we discovered one of Callie's favorite songs was on the tape.

Other Chinese language and music cassettes or CD's include *Chinese for Children* by Wendy Lin, and *Play and Learn Chinese with Mei Mei*.

"*Language Littles*" are bilingual dolls available in Spanish, Mandarin Chinese, Russian and more. Each sixteen-inch doll speaks between twenty-five and thirty phrases in English and another language. New dolls are currently being added to this collection. www.languagelittles.com/home_content

Large Toys and Outdoor Toys

Most children enjoy a rocking horse, play table and chairs, an art easel, or a kitchen set. I especially like a kitchen set and found that many toddlers will play with one for hours.

Callie enjoys jumping on a mini trampoline and has used it so much that she has built up very strong muscles in her legs. Other outdoor toys that are fun for toddlers include a swing set, play pool, and sandbox complete with bucket and pail. Wagons, push cars, and tricycles are other favorites.

Toys to Take

You will need to take at least two or three toys for your daughter to play with on your adoption trip. Great toys to take include:

Backpack

Beach Ball

Board books

Bubbles

Plastic keys

Purse

Small baby toys (assorted)

Soft doll

Stacking cups

Rattle

Chapter 8

Child Safety

There are many ways to protect your child from harm. Common sense and child awareness can be two of your best lines of defense. While it is impossible to eliminate the threat of accidents completely, you can significantly reduce the opportunity for dangerous and potentially life-threatening conditions. It is your responsibility as a parent to do so.

Keep the telephone numbers for your pediatrician, poison control center, Ask-a-Nurse programs, local emergency response line, and other related services posted close to the telephone.

Children are inquisitive by nature but lack an understanding of cause and effect. It takes just a few seconds for a child to get into trouble. Seemingly harmless conditions that can increase your daughter's risk for accident include the following:

- Busy time of day
- Change in routine or caregivers
- Death in the family
- Hunger (the hour before dinnertime)
- New addition to the family (child or pet)
- New home
- One or both parents out of town
- Parent(s)/caretaker(s) who are preoccupied: talking on the telephone, watching
- TV or working on the computer
- Parental stress

- Parents or caregivers in the bathroom
- Parents separating, divorcing or experiencing marital difficulties
- Pregnancy
- Preparing for, traveling to, and being on vacation
- Sibling has recently had an accident resulting in injury or broken bones
- Sick parent or siblings

Danger Zones

To childproof your home, start by placing any breakables, collectibles, and dangerous or irreplaceable items out of your child's reach. Toilets, stairs, and electrical appliances pose a great threat to your child, as do medications and household cleaners. The most common accidents for children include; climbing, poisoning, drowning, auto accidents, cuts and abrasions.

Zone 1: Medications

All medications should have childproof lids and should be kept safely out of reach. Medicine cabinets are unsafe because they rarely lock and can be reached by a climbing toddler. Sharp objects like scissors, razors, and pins should be removed from unlocked medicine cabinets.

Zone 2: Water

Toilets, tubs, whirlpools, and buckets or other water-filled containers, including ice chests and diaper pails, all pose a threat to your toddler. Buckets that hold five gallons or more are the most dangerous. Toddlers are top-heavy and can get stuck in any of these receptacles. You should never leave children unattended in a bath or near any body of water. It only takes a few inches of water to drown in.

Zone 3: Edibles

Many common household cleaners are poisonous if ingested. To minimize the risk of children ingesting these substances, always keep cleaning supplies in a securely locked area. These also need to be kept out of reach while you are using them. It has been traditionally recommended to keep syrup of ipecac handy to induce vomiting. However, some new research discounts the use of ipecac. BE sure to keep the poison control hot line number posted and ALWAYS call the hot line, before you give your child ipecac, or anything else that may induce vomiting. Some poisons may do more damage if regurgitated.

Leaving the most cautious child alone even for a few minutes when using household cleaners could be dangerous. Toddlers can be easily tempted by the pretty blue window cleaner that looks like the fruity drink the nice person brings them at the restaurant. Cocktails, beer, or wine are also fair game for small children and could result in intoxication or an alcohol overdose. Always empty glasses when you finish and teach toddlers that they are not to drink after other people.

Zone 4: The Garage

When you childproof your home, don't forget the garage. Paint, pesticides, and fertilizers can be toxic if ingested. Tools should also be left unplugged and out of reach. If you have an automatic garage door opener, check to see how well the doorstops and what size triggers it. I saw a test on television that suggested putting a cantaloupe or other melon where the garage door closes. If the melon is crushed, the garage door is a safety threat to your child.

Zone 5: Climbing

As your daughter enters the climbing stage, anything she can step on, pull up on, or climb on top of is potentially dangerous. Stairs should have gates at the top as well as the bottom. Bookcases, dressers, or other pieces of furniture should be bolted to the wall if it they are not secure enough to prevent your toddler from pulling them.

I use what I call the "finger test." I placed four fingers from each hand approximately 1½ to 2 inches from the edge of the furniture in question. If I think the furniture could be pulled over with the light amount of pressure I applied, then I took safety precautions. It was just my luck that the only piece of furniture I deemed unsafe in our house was the tall dresser in the nursery.

Zone 6: Electrical Appliances

Electrical appliances should always be turned off after use and kept out of reach. A toddler should never be allowed to touch an electrical appliance in the bathroom (hair dryer, curling iron, etc.) or in any other area that is close to water. Appliances that are plugged in do not have to be turned on to cause electrocution if they are exposed to or submerged in water. Irons can remain hot after use and should never be left on an ironing board. When moving a hot iron to a secured area, make sure the electrical cord is not left dangling and is also out of reach. Electrical cords for lamps, appliances, and so on, should be hidden or out of reach. This will prevent your daughter from pulling appliances on top of herself or possibly getting cut or burned.

Home Safety

No home could be properly childproofed without a variety of safety devices. You will have to assess your surroundings to determine which items best suit your needs. Items you may need to childproof your home include:

- Baby monitor
- Childproof patio door lock
- Choke tube
- Cord wind-ups
- Corner guards
- Door alarms
- Doorknob guards
- Door locks
- Doorstops
- Drawer locks
- Fire extinguisher
- Nonskid tub mats
- Outlet covers
- Playpen
- Power strip safety cover
- Safety gate/stair guard
- Screen guard
- Skid-resistant/tip-resistant stepstool
- Smoke alarm
- Stove guard

- Stove knob covers
- Toilet lid lock
- Tub spout covers
- VCR guard

Socket Safety

Outlet covers should cover electrical sockets. I recently saw a power outlet without covers next to a sink. Since this is well within reach of wet little hands, it is an accident waiting to happen.

If you use power strips, invest in a power strip safety cover. Cord wind-ups will help prevent children from pulling on electrical cords or pulling electrical appliances over.

Doors and Windows

If you have louvered doors or doors without locks, you may need to invest in door locks to keep toddlers out of these rooms or closets. Kid-proof patio door locks are also available for screen doors, which frequently do not have locks.

Safety gates can be used to prevent access to any restricted areas of your home. They may be used for doorways, hallways, or stairs.

Check window screens. I was at a friend's house recently when the screen fell out of one of her windows. You may need to purchase screen guards to prevent children from falling out or climbing out of windows.

Venetian blinds should have cord wind-ups installed so your daughter cannot become tangled in excess cord.

You may need door lock covers so that your daughter cannot lock herself in or you out of a room. This happens more often in a bathroom than any other room. This will of course present a whole other set of dangers, especially if you are visiting someone else's home. Toddlers are sometimes able to lock a door but have trouble unlocking it. I was once locked out of a house by a three-year-old that I was babysitting. It took a lot of coaxing to be allowed back into the house. If your daughter climbs out of bed at night or if she is a sleepwalker, all doors leading to the outside need door lock covers.

If you have a security system in your home, you may want to consider door alarms. They will tell you when someone enters or leaves the house and which door they are using. This will prevent toddlers from escaping unnoticed.

The Bathroom

No bathroom would be complete without a fair amount of safety devices. You should purchase a toilet lid lock to help keep toddlers out of the toilet, and your bathtub should have faucet covers and nonskid tub mats. These will help prevent falls and injury from bumping their heads. Most likely your daughter will need a stepstool to reach the sink. Stepstools should be skid- and tip-resistant. Medicine cabinets as well as other cabinets or drawers that contain household cleaners, medication, baby products (don't forget about any that may be in your daughter's bedroom), cosmetics, razors, scissors should have drawer and cabinet locks.

The Kitchen

Stove knob covers prevent your daughter from being able to turn the stove off or on. When cooking, use back burners whenever possible so toddlers won't be tempted to grab pot handles. When our daughter was in the hospital after she had her palate repaired, there was another child in the hospital who had pulled a pot of green beans on top of himself, resulting in serious burns. A stove guard could have prevented that accident.

Drawer and cabinet locks and latches should be used anywhere there are items that could cause injury to a toddler. Cutlery, scissors, or other sharp objects should be out of reach. If your daughter has ever been in a situation where not having enough food to eat was an issue, you may need to put a lock on the pantry to prevent unsupervised bingeing or "stealing" food.

Corner Guards

Corner guards are especially important in preventing injuries to small children. Coffee tables, end tables, and countertops can cause injury if a toddler hits her head on one. A neighbor's child hit her head on the corner of a piano and ended up starting school with two black eyes. The school called the Department of Social Services, and it led to an investigation.

Choke Tube

One way to test whether an object is too small for your daughter to play with or needs to be stored out of his reach is to test it in a choke tube. A choke tube is an acrylic tube that helps determine what represents a choking hazard. If the object will fit into the tube, it could be a choking hazard. Many small items are marked "not for children under 3." Because internationally adopted children may be small for their age or developmentally behind, you may need to consider if your daughter is big enough or mature enough to play with these items as they were intended.

VCR Guard

One of the newest child safety products is the VCR guard. Actually this item is really a VCR safety device since it protects the VCR from your child! A VCR guard will prevent your daughter from inserting movies incorrectly or other foreign objects into the VCR.

Fire Safety

All homes should have smoke detectors and fire extinguishers. Check periodically to make sure they are in working order. All children's pajamas should be flame resistant. Pajamas should fit snugly and be free of damage like rips or tears or missing or loose buttons. It is much safer for your child to sleep in pajamas rather than T-shirts or other favorite articles of clothing. Your home should have window decals alerting rescue personnel that there are children or pets in the home. These decals are usually available from the fire department.

The Playpen

If for some reason you need to divert your complete attention to something besides your toddler, a playpen can be used temporarily to keep her out of trouble. Although you would not want to leave her in the playpen for any length of time, it can come in handy if the phone rings, your dinner is burning, or you need to go to the bathroom. We have a portable playpen that also makes a great little travel bed. It also keeps toddlers from wandering off in a strange place.

Portable playpens, often come with travel bags, and make great travel beds. Most are easy to fold and convert from a play area to a bassinet. They may include a changing table and station, complete with diaper stacker. Bassinets can generally be used up to fifteen pounds. With out the bassinet, portable playpens like cribs, are usually only recommended until the child reaches thirty-four or thirty-five inches tall.

Car Seats

Car seats are not usually used in China. Because of this and the logistics involved in transporting a car seat to China, most adoptive families choose not to use one when they travel to complete their adoption. You will however need one when you return home.

When selecting a new car seat, make sure the one you select meets federal motor vehicle safety standards. If you will be using the car seat on an airplane, it should meet FAA requirements. Five-point harnesses provide more protection than three-point harnesses. According to the American Academy of Pediatrics, "Do not use shield boosters for children under 40 pounds, even if they are labeled for use at a lower weight."

Toddlers and young children should always ride in weight-appropriate car seats. When choosing a car seat for your toddler, you may want to consider how long your child will be able to use it and if it can be handed down to a younger sibling. We were lucky because the car seat we chose could be used for children weighing five to forty pounds. Since our daughter was almost thirty pounds when we adopted her, she was not able to use it for very long. However, our second addition did, and we moved Callie to a new car seat just prior to his arrival which coincided with the time she outgrew hers.

Car seats are safest when placed in the backseat. If possible, use the middle seat; it is the safest. A significant amount of car seats are installed incorrectly. To protect your child, have your car seat installation checked by an expert. Many police departments, fire departments, and automobile companies provide this service for free. Even when your toddler is buckled into a car seat, there is no guarantee that he can't escape. Teach your toddler proper etiquette for riding in a car: no screaming, no throwing things, and keep the seat belt on. You may want to keep a towel handy to cover any metal or plastic that could become hot while your car is sitting in the sun.

Car seats should provide infant head support or have a headrest, a five-point harness, adjustable height and weight position, adjust to rear and front facing positions as needed with adjustable reclining seats. It should also have adjustable handles, a stay in car adjustable base, a level indicator for proper installation.

We bought a car seat under mat help protect the car from accidents; it has a mesh pocket to store toys or other essentials. We also were given a baby view mirror. It has a suction cup that attaches to the windshield and allows you to see into the backseat so you can check on your toddler as often as needed. Most have washable fabric seat covers and many have cup holders.

Booster seats are usually not recommended until a child reaches thirty or forty pounds. They offer a three-point harness or side should straps, depending on the child's size. Most seats have cup and snack holders along with removable, washable seat pads. Many have some type of storage pockets for toys.

Toddlers—or infants, for that matter—should *never* be left alone in a car—even for a few minutes—and keys should never be left in the ignition. When you load your car with groceries or other items, your child should always be the last thing that goes into the car.

At the airport a few months ago, I saw the Hammacher Schlemmer's "All-in-One Car Seat Stroller" for the first time and thought "Wow! I love it." This versatile car seat converts from a secure car/plane seat (forward-or rear-facing) into a sturdy, maneuverable stroller or booster seat. It adjusts for children from 5 to 40 lbs. and retails for approximately $199.00. Before flying, check with your airline for possible use.

Strollers

Choose a stroller that will provide your child with the best protection. The stroller you choose should have reclinable seats and an adjustable canopy. Most strollers have a three or five point harness for safety.

It should have a wide wheelbase to prevent tipping and have shock absorbing, all terrain, swivel, wheels. Check for under-seat storage, because hanging a purse or diaper bag on stroller handles can cause tipping.

The stroller should fold easily for storage and have comfort grip padded handles with adjustable heights. The frame should not have sharp edges or spaces that could trap fingers and toes. The stroller should also have durable straps that can be adjusted and opened easily only by adults. Brakes are also important to prevent the stroller from rolling.

Many great stroller accessories are also available, including drink holders, food trays, and holders for toys and other gadgets. Other optional features include saddlebags, large storage baskets, and will work with various other products.

When shopping for a stroller, check out its weight and ease of use. Will you be able to pick it up and use it on your own? This is especially important if you are adopting more than one child and need a double or triple stroller. If your children are infant and toddler age consider a double stroller, which includes a standard stroller seat, a space for older toddlers/kindergartners to stand, and a small bench seat. Depending on the size of your daughter and your needs, you may be able to purchase a convertible stroller/car seat, thus eliminating the need for two separate items.

I like using an umbrella stroller. We chose a modified, more durable "sport-utility stroller." It has a retractable canopy, a storage basket, eight-inch wheels, and it opens and closes easily.

Less expensive umbrella strollers are lightweight and can be kept in your car for quick and easy access and can be used alternately with a more heavy-duty stroller. They can be found in most discount or baby stores and usually retail for around $15 to $20. If you want to use an umbrella stroller during your adoption journey, they can easily be purchased in China.

Baby Carriers and Slings

Baby carriers, slings, and other baby-wearing devices are very popular. They can help bonding and attachment while making life more convenient for new parents. Parents of small toddlers should be able to use some of these products.

The Baby Bjorn front carrier is for birth to ten months or 8 to 33 pounds. While a front carrier may fit, it may be more constrictive than a small wiggley toddler would like.

Hip Hammocks or other slings help with the natural tendency to carry a child sideways on the hip. They are designed for a slightly older baby/toddler and can be used by children who are 14 to 35 pounds and two months to three years old.

Some baby carriers will adjust to size and should hold and support the child while providing you with proper back support for the carrier. A carrier should have a padded waist belt. Carriers should allow baby to face in or out while in front or be worn on your back. They should have a padded back and head rest and distribute babies weight evenly. Depending on your strength and stamina, it may be necessary to do back-strengthening exercises before using a baby carrier.

Use caution when wearing toddlers as they can and will pick up things that they are not supposed to. Toddlers are also more likely to wiggle, stand up, or try to get out of their carrier. Your child should not be able to get out of the restraints or slip through the leg holes. Carriers should have dual side entry with a ventilation system and easy to clean fabric.

Carriers or Backpack carriers may come in handy if you are doing a large amount of walking. Backpacks should have lightweight, steel frames with padded shoulder straps, rain shield, and 5-point harness. Bottle pockets, and zippered compartments for storage are nice extras.

Do not run with a baby in a carrier, this includes at the airport, trying to make your connecting flight. Avoid running while carrying a small child in any manner; it can cause shaken baby syndrome. You can, however, run while pushing them in a jog stroller.

Swings, Walkers and Entertainers

Most babies love to rock and swing. Indoor motorized swings have multiple, reclining seat positions, with dual speed action and a washable seat cover. Don't use this in place of rocking your daughter yourself, use this while you are cooking dinner, (or waiting for the Pizza Man), etc.

Depending on whether your daughter is old enough to sit securely by herself, is on the verge of pulling up to a standing position or beginning to walk, a stationary entertainer or a mobile walker may be just the thing to provide safe, fun, exercise and entertainment. They should adjust to height, fold easily for storage, and allow your daughter to rock, spin, and bounce while safely seated in the swivel seat.

Safety Harness

Harnesses for children should be used sparingly and with caution. Both parent and child should be attached to each other, rather than the parent holding a leash. Resist the urge to pull on the cord to prevent misconduct or to change directions. This could result in your child falling or receiving other injury.

Harnesses are useful if you are shopping, attending a crowded festival, at an amusement park, or have several small children to watch, or if your child has a tendency to run ahead and hide.

Safety harnesses are not appropriate to use when traveling overseas to complete an adoption. While they are somewhat controversial in the United States, they are considered completely inappropriate elsewhere and could result in an adoption backlash within your host country.

Safety Resources

You may request safety information from the following resources:

American Academy of Pediatrics, www.aap.org

> Web-site includes parenting, health topics, publications and bookstore, resources, advocacy, and a variety of on-line services.

> Tipp—The Injury Prevention Program: Information is available from the American Academy of Pediatrics on product safety, injury prevention, childproofing your home, and age related safety sheets.

> Car Safety Seats: A Guide to Families 2005
> www.aap.org/family/carseatguide.htm

Department of Transportation-Auto Safety Hotline (ASH): Call (800) 424-9153 for current information on child safety-seat recalls, safety notices, and replacement parts. www.nhtsa.dot.gov/hotline

Juvenile Products Manufacturers Association

> They have safety certification on many baby products, including information on cribs, high chairs, walkers, and stoppers. www.jpma.org
> JPMA
> 15000 Commerce Parkway
> Suite C
> Mt. Laurel, NJ, 08054
> 856-638-0420

Nationwide Poison Control Center: (800) 222-1222

U.S. Consumer Product Safety Commission

> Washington DC, 20207-0001
> Hot Line: (800) 638-2772

Chapter 9

A Safe Outdoors

Once you have childproofed your home, you will realize that the great outdoors presents a whole new set of problems. When outdoors, toddlers should never be left unsupervised. They should also be taught never to leave their specific play area without your permission.

If your yard is fenced, make sure all latches are in working order and that your toddler cannot unlatch them. At our house, we had imaginary lines at the sides of the house that Callie was not allowed past. We never allowed her in the front yard by herself when she was small.

Parking Lots and Streets

Set clear parameters for walking in parking lots and for crossing streets. Teach children not to play in the street or to cross the street by themselves. Always teach them to look left and right before crossing.

Our rules are simple:

1. No playing while getting in or out of the car, especially when it is dark.

2. You must hold a hand while in a parking lot or when you are crossing the street. If Callie refused to hold my hand in the parking lot, then she lost walking privileges. We would simply pick her up and carry her (sometimes kicking and screaming) either to the car or to the sidewalk.

Water Safety

Water poses a potential threat to your daughter, and she should never be left unattended in or near hot tubs, swimming pools, ornamental garden ponds, or even kiddy pools. Toddlers can drown in only a few inches of water. Always follow strict water safety rules:

1. Swimming pools should be equipped with appropriate life-saving devices.
2. Pool covers do not provide the necessary safety that a fenced-in pool area provides.
3. Do not rely on flotation devices to protect your child completely.
4. Children of all ages and swimming abilities still need adult supervision.
5. No running by the pool.
6. Small children must wear safety devices the entire time they are in the pool area not just while in the water.
7. Children are not allowed to stand on the edge of an adult pool and get things out or scoop out water.
8. Always remove toys, floats, and so on from the pool after use.
9. Teach children that they are not allowed in the pool or pool area without an adult.
10. Make sure there is always one adult present for every three children.

If you have a pool in your yard that has water over six feet deep and you cannot swim well enough to jump in after someone, then children should not be allowed in the pool area without an adult present who can.

Insects and Other Pests

Always take steps to protect your daughter from insects. Children may be quite intrigued by a variety of bugs and assorted creepy-crawlies. You may even be given one as a "gift." You can teach your child to identify friendly or harmless insects from those that could potentially bite or sting.

It may be necessary to use an insect repellant to protect your daughter from mosquitoes during summer months. It is important to follow the manufacturer's guidelines and rinse repellants off when children return indoors.

Because you may have very little family history, you may not know if your daughter has a predisposition to being allergic to bee stings or other insect bites. You may want to keep children's Benadryl on hand or consult your pediatrician on how to best prepare for such an event.

If your daughter has been bitten or stung and is developing a rash or hives, call your pediatrician and seek medical help immediately. She could be having a potentially life-threatening allergic reaction.

Playgrounds and Parks

Swing sets and jungle gyms are great ways for children to learn new skills and spend time with their peers. For Callie's fourth birthday, she was given a swing set. It did not take her long to master swinging and she can swing as high as it will go. (You will be grateful when your child learns this skill and you don't have to push!) Anchors are a safety necessity to prevent swing sets from flipping, and most manufacturers recommend using either wood chips, mulch, or sand under playground equipment. Periodically check for loose nuts, bolts, or anything that could catch clothing or hair.

Playground safety is much like teenagers learning the rules of the road. Teach toddlers to wait until it is their turn to go down a slide. Children should never stand on, climb up, or push someone down a slide. Swing safety includes no jumping from swings, no swinging on stomachs, no walking in front of or behind someone who is swinging, no pushing peers, and no twisting chains on the swing.

When visiting neighborhood parks, make sure that you keep your child in view at all times. Examine the area to make sure there are no areas that need repair or that could cause injury to your child. In summer months, check that equipment is not too hot to burn your child. If you see something that is a potential safety hazard, report it to park management.

Sandboxes should have fresh, clean sand and be free of sticks, leaves, and other debris. Always keep sandboxes covered when not in use. Don't let your daughter throw or eat sand, no matter how delicious the mud pies look.

Cats and Dogs

Pets are extremely scent-oriented. As soon as we got our travel date, I began wearing the baby lotion I had gotten for our daughter. My theory was that if our cat began associating this smell with me, when we arrived with our daughter he would be familiar with her scent and might more readily accept a new addition. I also closed the door to the nursery to get the cat used to not being able to spend time in that room.

Toddlers may not understand the difference between pet food and people food. This is especially true of dry cat food. Children who have experienced hunger or malnutrition may be especially attracted to pet food. If it is kept in an easily accessible area or where the pet has continual access to his food bowl, your daughter may consider it fair game the next time she's hungry. When my brother was small (I love telling this story), I caught him eating dry cat food. (Of course, I immediately told on him.) You may need to reconsider your pet's feeding rituals and food location.

As soon as our cat and our daughter became familiar with each other, I began the process of helping the two of them bond. I had always poured the cat's dry food directly into the bowl, which was sitting in its usual location. After our daughter arrived, I would pick up the food bowl and fill it up. After the bowl was full, I would give it to our daughter and help her give it to the cat. This served the dual purpose of teaching our daughter that this food was for the cat and of helping the cat accept her as a member of the family. Now Callie and our cat are good friends, and the cat will even let her brush him.

Dogs often pose more of a threat to children than cats. Although both can bite, dog bites can be much more serious. Cat scratches can be nasty and can leave scars; however, the most serious pet-related injuries usually are a result of dog attacks. Dogs are pack animals and must establish dominance over—or be submissive to—newcomers.

Children who are new to the home and pet or are visiting should never be left unattended with a dog. This is especially important for medium to large dogs or for species that tend to be more aggressive like Rottweilers, German shepherds, Doberman Pinschers, and so on. If you have or know of a dog that has bitten children before, you need to take steps to protect both your daughter and the pet.

In many states, emergency room personnel are required by law to report these incidences. They must then be investigated and require quarantine of the animal to ensure they do not have rabies. If the animal repeats its actions and bites another child, regardless of the circumstances, it will be put to sleep as required by law.

You should teach your daughter the following pet etiquette, or "petiquette" as I like to call it:

1. Ask a grownup for permission before approaching or petting an animal.
2. Avoid animals you do not know, and call a grownup if they approach you or enter your yard.
3. Never approach or touch a sleeping animal.
4. Never approach a mother animal with her babies without a grownup.
5. Do not touch an animal's food.
6. Do not poke an animal in the eyes.
7. Do not chase an animal that is running from you.
8. Leave fighting animals alone and call for a grownup.
9. If an animal is growling or angry, immediately stop what you are doing.

The first thing I do when I meet a new animal is to slowly reach out my hand and let him smell it. I figure that if he is clearly not interested, he will let me know by walking away or ignoring me. The correct way for a toddler to pet an animal is to rub it under the chin or to gently stoke his back. If a dog is growling or angry, the child should look down at his feet, take a step back and roll into a ball, covering his face with his arms. For an upset cat, the child should back away slowly. Usually a cat will then remove himself from the situation.

Other Animals

Cats and dogs are not the only pets that could pose a danger to your daughter. Hamsters, parakeets, lizards, skinks, monkeys, ferrets, rabbits, geese, and snakes will all bite. As a former zoo volunteer who helped with the two- and three-year-old classes, I know first-hand that toddlers have a natural tendency to go for animals' eyes. Eyes are located close to the mouth, and it is an animal's natural instinct to bite when it feels threatened. Virtually any animal cage that a toddler can get her fingers into can expose a toddler to potential injury.

Don't forget outdoor animals; this would include both wild animals and live-stock. Most wild animals will run when approached by humans. That doesn't mean that toddlers will not pursue them. Given the opportunity, most toddlers will try to pick up or pet wild animals.

Large predators like a mountain lion will look for the smallest prey, if they decide to pursue a group of humans. Never let your daughter run ahead or lag behind when hiking or walking on trails. However, if a bear approaches your child, she should curl up into a little ball on the ground. But if she is approached by a large feline, she should grab the hem of her jacket and raise both the jacket and her arms over her head. This will make her appear larger and should make the predator second-guess its attack.

Although livestock are domesticated, that doesn't mean accidents don't happen. Just the size difference between a toddler and a horse or cow is an accident waiting to happen. Also be aware of water sources. Is the livestock's primary water source a pond or large trough that a small child could get into? Is there a ladder in the barn leading to an open second level? Do electrical fences surround the animals, or can your daughter climb through the fence where the animals are?

Always be aware of your surroundings and potential hazards. Look for ways to prevent injuries. Teach your children to respect animals and their environment. Many zoos have classes available for toddlers and older children. These classes are a great way to introduce children to animals that they might not otherwise get the opportunity to meet.

Miscellaneous

Other potential hazards may include the following:

- Assorted tools (including garden tools)
- Buckets
- Chemicals for the pool
- Decks
- Driveway
- Electrical outlets
- Fences or gates
- Fertilizer, pesticides, or lawn chemicals
- Fireworks, including sparklers
- Holes
- Hot grills, matches, fire starters
- Lawnmowers
- Picnic tables, lawn chairs
- Plants, flowers, vegetables, berries

- Rocks
- Steps or ladders
- Trees (climbing)/tree houses
- Wells
- Woodpiles

Chapter 10

Mealtime Mania

I love toddlers. I love the way one day they will eat broccoli and the next day they won't. I love the way they say "yuck" when they try something new and how their version of trying a new food is to stick their tongue on it. I love their little pouty faces when you tell them no, how their eyes get as big as saucers when you bring them a present, and how they play with their silverware even when it regularly lands on the floor. I also love how you can make them laugh by just pretending to tickle them.

I believe that toddlers live in a world all their own. They are the center of their own universe, and we are the loyal subjects ready to attend to their every command. I have affectionately named this small kingdom of little people the Kingdom of Toddlerdom.

Not long before we adopted our daughter, a friend's toddler sat next to me at the dinner table and proceeded to scream "I want some juice" while kicking me under the table. What did we do? You guessed it; we got him some juice. Of course it didn't help that we had forgotten to get him something to drink.

Setting the Table

You will need some or all of the following:

- Baby bottles (three-8oz.)
- Bibs (3)
- Booster chair
- Bottle brush
- Bottle liners, one roll

- Bottle warmer
- Bottle drying rack
- Dinnerware
- Food storage containers
- High chair
- Insulated bottle tote
- Nipples—assorted-standard/long/straight
- Nipple adapter
- Place mat
- Silverware
- Snack cups
- Splat mat
- Training cups

Your daughter's age, development, and current diet will help determine your dining needs. She may have eaten only semisolid foods or may not have been exposed to many different foods. Young toddlers or special-needs toddlers may still be bottle-fed. On the other hand, children are weaned at an early age, and toddlers may have to learn how to use a sippy cup or straw.

The children at Callie's orphanage drank out of teacups. Because her cleft palate had not been repaired, Callie could not use a straw or a spill-proof cup if it had the spill-proof insert in place. Because of this, I did not know for several months that the insert was not supposed to be removed when in use.

Your daughter may never have eaten from a plate or used a fork. If the primary food was rice, then she may have only used a bowl and spoon for eating. She may never have fed herself, eaten with her fingers, or been allowed to touch her food. You will learn from trial and error.

For information baby travel needs, see Chapter 18, Packing for Your Trip: Essentials for Baby.

The High Chair

High chairs are usually recommended for children up to age three or who are thirty to forty pounds in weight. It should have a padded cloth seat which is removable and washable with an easy clean, dishwasher safe tray with removable inserts. A five-point harness system, along with reclining seat and multi height positions, will adjust to suit growing babies needs.

If you are adopting a toddler, don't buy one of those fancy, expensive high chairs that your she will not want to sit in after she figures out everyone else is in a big chair. The best buy for the amount of time you will use it is a four-way convertible high chair. The one that we purchased held an infant carrier. It also converted into a regular high chair. Once your child does not need to use the high chair tray and wants to sit at the table, the chair can be converted to a stand-alone booster chair and will also convert to a table and chair desk set, complete with a desk tray for storing crayons and paper.

When your daughter decides it is time to sit in a chair like a grownup (or other children), you may need to purchase a regular booster chair that will fit into your dining room chairs. Depending on the age or size of your daughter, you may be able to skip the high chair and purchase a booster chair. With Callie and Sean, both age three at the time of their adoption, we certainly could have.

The best product that we found was a portable booster seat. It folds for travel so I can take it with us when we go out to dinner, on vacation, or to dinner at a friend's. Booster seats should have a removable, easy to clean feeding tray, multi height adjustment, with a three-point harness system for safety.

Spills Happen

The single, most important mealtime necessity is the Splat Mat. No matter what the seating arrangement is there will be spills and dropped food. This mat will save your carpet or flooring and make cleanup simple. Simply put this plastic floor cover beneath your daughter's seat and presto! An anti-carpet-cleaning device.

Short of an all-out food fight, your flooring will probably be spared. However, that dropped peanut butter and jelly sandwich may not always land where it is most convenient. If your home is carpeted, you will want to invest in a good spot remover.

The phrase "you are what you eat" must have came from the mother of a toddler. Toddlers, especially young toddlers who may be trying lots of new foods, will frequently wear their dinner. Your budding artist will love to touch, taste, finger-paint, and sculpt with her food.

Bibs will help protect and keep clothes clean. Cloth bibs can be thrown in the wash while waterproof bibs can be wiped off with a clean damp cloth. Disposable bibs are the latest invention; they would be great for traveling.

Of course any new parent knows that once a spot has made its way onto your beloved daughter's clothing, the clothes should be changed. Wrong! You will learn to overcome this temptation. It's okay. You will get used to it. You do not have to change your daughter's clothes immediately; at the rate of two or three shirts or outfits a day, you will soon learn that "spills happen."

Table Manners

Table manners will vary. Both Callie and her friend Victoria had great table manners when they came home. However, this did not last long for either child. Once they discovered that mealtime is a pleasant experience, where there are a variety of foods and there is always enough, their table manners deteriorated and they began to behave more like typical toddlers.

Your child may have had to fight to protect her food from other children, or she may have been an aggressor. Callie wanted all of her dinnerware to touch. She would eat all the crumbs off the table and wanted those on the floor as well. At first she would eat everything, but once she learned that she had options, there was always enough food, and she did not have to eat things she did not like, she became much more selective.

Victoria would put her arm around her plate as to not allow anyone else to get close, and Callie once pulled a hamburger out of my hand after I had taken it from her because the meat was about to fall out. For children in orphanages, mealtime is a serious business.

A turning point for Callie was when she would eat a dozen or so bites and want to be excused. The small amount of food took the edge off of her hunger, and because she could comprehend the difference between being hungry and knowing true hunger, she did not want to finish her dinner. At that point she was confident that there was always enough food and that if she was hungry, she would be fed.

Once your child forgets how crucial eating was to her basic survival, she should relax and eating should become a more pleasurable experience.

Food and Attachment

Food is the most essential element in creating attachment. Although most toddlers are capable to a certain degree of feeding themselves, adopted toddlers should not be allowed to do this until parents have established themselves as the primary food provider and caretaker.

When possible, parents should always be the ones who feed their child, no matter how resistant the child may be. This may include regressing to the bottle stage; sitting in the parent's lap and eating from the parent's plate; the parent feeding and holding silverware while the child is eating; and discontinuing feeding for a short time while the parent continues to eat if the child refuses to allow the parent to feed him.

Attachment inhibitors could include toddlers eating without their parents' help, being left to eat by themselves even if the parents are in the room with them, denial of food as a punishment, or possibly being forced to eat everything on their plate.

Feeding Your Baby

Feeding your baby and making dining a pleasant experience is an integral part of bonding and attachment. Find out as much as possible about your child's current diet, her likes and dislikes as well as any allergies that she may have. Chances are that there are many common foods that your daughter may never have experienced. She may also like some foods that you cannot imagine any child or even yourself eating.

Older infants who can sit without support, roll around, eat from a spoon, and swallow without problems most likely still need a variety of baby foods. These foods could include formula, baby cereal, juice, and a variety of baby foods. You may also need to consider single-flavored baby food as a starting point and work your way up to mixed foods.

If you arrive to find your baby is still drinking formula, you may wish to buy the one they are using at the orphanage. It may be easier to make the transition at home and then switch to milk based formula. Some pediatricians recommend an iron fortified, milk based formula for babies while others recommend a lactos-free formula for babies adopted from China. Most babies tolerate either equally well, as lactose problems in Asian children typically do not manifest until a later age. Soy based formulas may cause constipation.

Powdered formula will pack easiest; 4-5 cans should be plenty. You will need a thermos or some type of bottle warmer, to take with you when you venture out. The hot water in your room, which is in thermos, should be safe to use for baby.

Whichever type bottles you choose to take, washable or disposable, make sure that the nipples are interchangeable and that you take a variety of sizes, with different type openings, and textures. Your daughter will choose which one she prefers and this may change over the course of your trip. You may also need to enlarge holes on nipples to accommodate these changes.

If your daughter refuse to eat, then try different nipples and temperatures of formula. Most likely she will want it very hot, but you may be able to decrease the temperature as her comfort level with you increases. It may also be necessary to play with the strength of the formula, and you may want to start with a higher concentrate of water than is recommended as she is getting accustomed to her new formula. In some cases children are used to a sweeter formula so adding sugar may help.

Feeding Your Toddler

Toddlers who are learning to crawl can pull themselves up, drink from a cup, eat with their fingers, and mash food with their gums. They are probably not ready for adult food but will enjoy foods that can be chewed and swallowed easily. Baby foods such as meat and pasta or chicken and rice will offer more variety, flavor, and textures than puréed or single-flavored foods will.

Older toddlers usually have teeth and can bite easily. They can walk with or without help. Most likely they have learned to drink from a cup and can use a spoon. They can eat bite-size food and will chew before swallowing. These toddlers should be able to enjoy a variety of foods including cereal, bread, milk, juice, yogurt, cookies, soups, stews, sliced fruit, sliced raw or cooked vegetables, meat cut into small pieces, pasta, and many other table foods.

Callie had to learn to eat vegetables and immediately loved but had never been given juice. We had been told that she liked meat and sweets. She also loves bread but has since decided that she does not care for traditional Russian food such as beets or pickles which our son loves above all else.

For months I tried to make mashed potatoes to her liking. Every time we ate baked potatoes, I would mash hers. I tried adding dill and sour cream and experimented with different thickness with a varying degree of results. Finally one day she sat down with her grandmother and started eating a regular baked potato. Who would have thought?

Taste, texture, smell, temperature (to hot or too cold) presentation, and experience will play an important role in your child's eating habits. Callie was so excited the first time I made a boiled egg, but she was picky about how they were cut. She wants boiled eggs to be cut in half horizontally instead of in vertical quarters. She also would not eat scrambled eggs until I started adding a little butter to the pan.

Your toddler may go through a phase where she wants to eat the same thing for lunch every day, eats only green food, or must have ketchup on everything. These are typical toddler eating patterns. You may have to teach your child decision-making and how to choose what they would like to eat. Experimentation is the key to feeding your new toddler.

Feeding Problems

Feeding problems can include upset stomach, allergies, food obsessions, over-eating, or refusing to eat. Feeding techniques, wrong size nipples on bottles, use of spoons, feeding position (person feeding them is facing them instead of sitting behind them), and dining environment resulting in over-stimulation, all can contribute to eating difficulties. Because feeding and attachment are so closely interwoven, have a full medical evaluation once you arrive home. Address any feeding concerns with your pediatrician or specialist. Children may require an intervention program or possible occupational or feeding therapy. Common feeding problems can include the following:

Sensitive Tummies: Once you receive custody of your daughter, she will experience many things for the first time. Travel, time change, and a change in caretakers all will affect your daughter. This will include many new foods. Start slowly and play it safe. The introduction of new foods is an upset stomach waiting to happen.

The first night Callie spent with us, we were given kefir for an evening snack and told to give her this for breakfast as well. Mommy decided that when in Russia, do as the Russians do. So no kefir for breakfast since I had meat and potatoes in the fridge. We'd had meat and potatoes all week for breakfast; surely this would be far better than the lumpy, brown, rotten-yogurt-looking stuff.

That was only my first mistake; apple juice for a drink, and more apple juice on the plane were the second and third. What followed was not pretty. Airsickness, carsickness, and motion sickness were my christening as a new mother.

Allergies: Approximately 25 percent of children may have some types of food allergies. Symptoms can include runny nose, asthma, colic, rashes, or crankiness. Many times allergies are inherited, but this information will be unavailable. You will have to use caution.

Until you are home, avoid highly allergic foods such as milk or dairy products, eggs, corn, wheat, soy, citrus, peanuts or peanut butter, sugar, chocolate, tomatoes, pork, and shellfish. Your daughter's caretaker should be able to give you information about any known allergies. If your daughter is already drinking milk or milk products, chances are they will not produce an allergic reaction.

Introducing one new food at a time will help identify food allergies. Foods that are least likely to produce an allergic reaction are apples, peaches, pears, broccoli, cauliflower, carrots, sweet potatoes, rice, chicken, salmon, and turkey.

Food Sensitivities: These may include sensitivity to food coloring, preservatives, sugar, and other stimulants. Your daughter may have limited exposure to any number of these and may experience hyperactivity, over stimulation, crankiness, and irritability. These reactions may mimic the affect of Attention Deficit Disorder and Attention Deficit Hyperactivity Disorder.

Avoid chocolate, beverages that contain caffeine, and foods with red and blue dyes. Juice, cereal, and other snacks can be overloaded with many of these irritants. Good basics are cheese crackers, simple cereals, animal crackers, and other simple low-sugar snack foods. Do not use low-fat products. Use whole milk, if your child is not drinking formula. Include 100% fruit juice, fresh fruits and vegetables and as many all-natural products as possible in your child's diet.

Depending upon who you ask and what research you find, you may be told that Asian children are more susceptible to lactose intolerance. While this may or may not be true it is something to keep in mind if you suspect your daughter may be having problems with milk products. If so it may be necessary for her to drink soymilk.

Hoarding and Bingeing: Children who are malnourished, experience hunger, or have a fear of being hungry may hoard, steal, or binge after adoption. Malnourished or children who have been abused by having food withheld are more susceptible to having food-related issues. While some children will eat until they make themselves sick, others may show no interest in food.

Children who have food related issues might have to have their food regulated. For older children it may be necessary to lock cupboards, leave a tray of healthy snacks accessible at all times or to find other positive ways to reinforce the fact that food will always be available. It is necessary that your daughter receive proper diet and nutrition. Parents must determine their child's needs versus their wants.

Sensory Integration: Lack of stimulation and underdeveloped senses can result in tactile and auditory processing problems called sensory integration disorder. This disorder can include problems with auditory processing and hyper- or hyposensitivity to noise, touches, or sight. This sensitivity may manifest as an oral aversion to food, including problems with taste or texture, underdeveloped muscles used for chewing, or sucking, or swallowing, accepting foods, or simply having food in the mouth.

The theory that "when she gets hungry enough, she'll eat" may not apply to children with a sensory integration oral aversion to food. Children who have low muscle tone in facial muscles, experienced poor feeding techniques or have related behavioral or emotional problems must learn to eat. One mother in an adoption group told me that when her child was adopted he was slowly starving himself to death and no one in the orphanage would make him eat. She also told me she once held his mouth closed for forty-five minutes so he would not spit his food out. Ultimately she prevailed.

The degree of seriousness may vary, and many children who have sensory integration issues may happily eat a limited diet. Trying new foods, particularly with different textures, however, can be a problem. Consult your pediatrician at once if you suspect your child's eating problems are more than a dislike of the food she is being given. You may be refereed to an occupational therapist or pediatric feeding specialist.

Chapter 11

Bath Time

Whoever wrote the nursery rhyme "Rub-a-dub-dub, three men in a tub" forgot to mention the real reason they were all in the tub: It takes six hands to give a toddler a bath! One to keep them in the tub, one to hold the washcloth, one to pour the soap and shampoo, one to lather and rinse, one to prevent injury and one to keep them entertained.

Of course three men equals one Mommy, but Callie's first bath was given to her by her father. I hate to admit this publicly, but I was quite impressed that he had taken it upon himself, while I was last minute shopping. Callie loved the bath, but that's not to say that there haven't been some moments since then!

Memories of Bath Times Past

Each child will come with bath experiences, which will vary greatly depending on the age and situation she was in prior to adoption. It is also possible that the only bathing that your daughter received was a cold shower or from a wash-basin with a washcloth. While baths should be pleasant experiences, they may have been just the opposite for your daughter.

She may want to stand up in the tub and may not understand the concept of sitting down. You will need to exercise extra caution during this adjustment period. Regardless, never leave your daughter alone, even if she has no problems sitting up.

Bathing Baby

On your adoption trip to China you may want to take an infant travel bathtub. Some are a sponge base or foam cushion that can sit in a sink or adult bathtub. Others are stand alone, inflatable blow-up tubs, which could be used on a counter top or in a tub. Some baby bathtubs will convert to a bath seat, and should fold for storage. Most are mildew resistant.

Tips for making bath time pleasant for baby include:

1. Start slow and build trust.
2. Make sure the water is warm.
3. Don't fill the tub all the way.
4. Hold or support your baby while bathing her.
5. Speak softly or sing to her.
6. Make eye contact.
7. Include a toy or two.
8. Use mild soap.
9. Wash with soft sponge or washcloth.
10. Don't let the water get to cold, or let the baby catch a chill.
11. Use warm towels.
12. Pat gently to dry.

The Bath-Resistant Baby

Adopted children who may not have been bathed regularly or are resistant to touch, may be terrified of the bath during the adjustment period. While bathing a bath-resistant child can be frustrating and emotionally draining, it is actually a good opportunity to strengthen your attachment. Your daughter will come to trust that bathing is a pleasant experience.

If your child is bath-resistant, you may have to bathe with her (some people choose to wear swimsuits to do this) or have her in the room with you while you bathe in order to familiarize her with being bathed in or around the tub. It may take a child several months before becoming comfortable with sitting in the tub. Naturally, bath toys can be good enticements.

Bath Essentials

Here are the bath essentials:

- Bath sponges
- Bath toys
- Brush, comb
- Bubble bath
- Diaper ointment
- Diapers, underwear
- Faucet covers
- Lotion
- Nail clippers
- Nonskid mat
- Pajamas
- Shampoo
- Soap
- Swivel or Suction Bath Rings
- Talcum powder
- Toothbrush, toothpaste (Finger toothbrush for babies)
- Towels, hooded towels
- Washcloths

Before you start the bath, always check the water temperature. Water that may be the perfect temperature for you may be too hot for your daughter, especially if you are like my friend who likes her bathwater so hot it turns her skin pink! Water temperature should be warm enough to stay warm for the duration of the bath without causing discomfort.

A nonskid tub mat will help prevent falls, and faucet covers can help prevent scalding and head injuries. Swivel or suction bath seats or rings should be used only if your daughter can sit up by herself. Again, never leave your daughter unattended while in the bath.

You probably would not want or need to purchase a bath seat or ring unless your child is a young toddler or has special needs. There's also a good possibility that you may not be able to use a bath seat. This will depend on your child's comfort level in the tub.

Other bath essentials include washcloths (I like animal-shaped ones) or bath sponges and towels or hooded towels. Use soap and shampoo for babies with sensitive skin until you can determine if your daughter has any allergies. Shampoo should be gentle enough for little eyes, and depending on your daughter's hair type or length, you may need a no-tangles formula.

Restrict the use of bubble bath to older toddlers. Use sparingly, especially for little girls who can be more susceptible to urinary tract infections.

Of course all children can tell you that baths are no fun without toys, and there are a wide variety to choose from. I prefer ones that can dry easily, and I shy away from bath books or cloth bath toys that need to be washed frequently because they can harbor germs. Callie's favorite bath toys included her bath blocks and a bath baby doll.

Toys should always be developmental and age-appropriate. A toy shelf is a great place to store bath toys. They stay tidy and are usually designed so that the water will drain off the toys.

After you dry off your daughter, she will most likely streak across the house naked (or jump up and down on the bed). If you are fast enough to catch her before this happens, you will be able to add any lotions, powders, or ointments; diaper her or put on underwear; put pajamas on; clip and file fingernails; brush, comb and dry her hair; and brush her teeth. If you have to chase your child thought the house, you will still need to complete the ablutions upon her capture—but then you can have some quiet cuddle time. Reading to your daughter will help her unwind before bedtime.

Don't Forget to Brush Her Teeth

Your daughter has never had her teeth brushed. If she is a baby or toddler, she may have had them washed with a washcloth or similar device. You may need to purchase a finger toothbrush as opposed to a standard child's toothbrush. A finger toothbrush looks like a plastic finger puppet, which is textured. It is worn by the parent, who in turn cleans babies teeth with.

Poor dental care, lack of water with fluoride, little milk, no vitamins, all compounded by drinking very sweet tea and no dentist may all contribute to poor dental hygiene.

Once you are home, settled in, are into a routine and have completed your initial visits with the pediatrician, you may want to schedule a dental visit. Do not wait if you have any reason for concern.

Chapter 12

Diaper Care and Potty Training

The age of your daughter will determine her diapering needs. If she is in diapers, you will have to decide between cloth and disposable diapers. The biggest advantages to using disposable diapers seem to be that they absorb moisture and keep wetness away from baby's skin. They also fit more securely and you can throw them away rather than having to wash them or use a diaper service. One disadvantage is that they do not promote potty training because the child does not feel as much discomfort at having a wet or dirty diaper.

Changing a Diaper

When my husband and I began the adoption process, we had no clue how to change a diaper. For diaper changes, you will need the following:

- Clean diapers
- Diaper cream or petroleum jelly
- Disposable diaper wipes
- A change of clothes if necessary

Now here's how to change a diaper:

1. Remove the dirty diaper and use diaper wipes to clean the baby. For little girls, wipe from the front to the back. This is important to help prevent urinary tract infections. Little boys have great aim so be sure to drape them with a clean diaper. Throw away the dirty disposable diaper and wipes in an odorless diaper pail.

2. If needed, use diaper rash cream or petroleum jelly as directed by your pediatrician.

3. Put on the new diaper according to the instructions on the diaper package.

Diaper Details

Plan on using an average of four to six diapers a day. For a total of approximately 100 diapers on your adoption trip. You should be able to purchase disposable diapers in most places; however, you probably want to take enough to last you a few days, as they may be hard to find in more rural areas. Diapers cost more in China and it may be hard to find Ultra thin in smaller cities.

You will use an average of ten to twelve baby wipes a day. You will need between fifty and one hundred baby wipes total. You need to plan on bringing most of the wipes that you will need. Soft-sided refills travel better than the plastic boxes.

Diaper Disposal

You will want a diaper disposal that will lock odor in. They generally hold twenty five to thirty diapers. Most use standard trash bags and can be used for disposable or cloth diapers.

To dispose of soiled diapers while you are in China, take disposable diaper bags or use gallon freezer bags to seal in odor between housekeeping visits.

Diaper Rash

If your daughter is coming from an orphanage, she may not have had her diaper changed as frequently as preferred and she may have developed a nasty case of diaper rash. Get a pediatrician's recommendation on how to treat diaper rash ahead of time. It can be very painful. The following tips can help soothe diaper rash:

•   Change the diaper as soon as your daughter soils it. Do not use baby powder.

•   If possible, let your daughter go bare-bottomed for a time. The air will help dry out the diaper rash.

- Do not use plastic pants or disposable diapers if possible. They can make diaper rash worse.
- Wash baby with soap and water; baby wipes can cause additional irritation.

Circumcision

If you are adopting a boy, he has most likely not been circumcised. If you wish to consider circumcision, you will need to speak to your pediatrician. She can discuss the advantages and disadvantages as well as answer any questions that you may have. She may refer you to a pediatric urologist. In most cases, circumcision is considered cosmetic surgery (unless it is medically necessary) and health insurance usually will not cover the cost of the procedure. Check with your insurance provider.

Potty Training

Your daughter may have already started potty training. How a child has been potty trained and at what age will vary. Your adoption agency may recommend that you bring a potty chair with you when you travel to adopt your child. If your child is between twelve and thirty-six months, skip the potty-chair and just plan on using disposable diapers or disposable training pants. Most likely she is not truly potty trained but was put on the potty to go at certain times of the day. In group settings, children often have little flexibility in their schedules and are expected to go to the bathroom to comply with their regimented schedule. If she misses her window of opportunity, she will have an accident. Most likely, she will not have the communication skills or understand the concept of going when she needs to.

You may need to take a potty-chair with you when you travel to adopt older toddlers who would be more secure in their potty training. You may also be able to buy a potty-chair or you may be able to get away with taking a potty seat rather than a potty-chair. A potty seat fits on top of a toilet seat and is much smaller than a whole chair. This may or may not work. Using a potty seat may be a problem in places where toilets are more like latrines. When we were in Russia, everywhere we went had a different type of toilet. Flushing was an adventure because the handles were in different places on different toilets. All the toilets were shaped a little differently, and they did not really have seats as we know them. We could not have used a potty seat even if we needed to.

If your daughter is closer to thirty-six months, you should be able to skip taking a potty-chair with you on your trip. You would however need to take disposable training pants or cotton training pants for children ages three to six. Disposable training pants can be pulled up and down just like regular underwear but will help prevent accidents. Make sure they come apart at the side. If they don't, it can be really messy if your daughter has diarrhea. This is especially important when changes of diet and travel are occurring or if your child has to sleep with you. Also take either a few pairs of cotton training pants or regular children's underwear in case your daughter is used to wearing it and refuses to wear the disposable diapers.

Children who are in the process of potty training or who are potty trained may regress when life-altering changes are made. This occurs in children who aren't adopted as well as adopted ones.

Our daughter used a potty-chair at the orphanage, but she did not get to decide when she went to the bathroom. She especially enjoyed exercising her newfound independence. She quickly learned that she received an immediate response to her expressing a need to relieve herself. We would sometimes have to take her to the bathroom four or five times during dinner. She enjoyed the cause and effect: She decides that "I am bored so I want to get up, maybe play in the sink while washing my hands...I can sit with Aunt Kathy when I come back, I am scared and want to leave, etc."

Fortunately most of the novelty has worn off, but she will still try on occasion if she is bored. We have to determine if she is faking or really needs to go. Just be flexible—accidents will happen.

Chapter 13

The Medicine Cabinet

As with any medication, consult your physician before giving medication to your children. In your initial consultation with your pediatrician, he or she will give you recommendations on which medication to use as well as when and how to use it. Always follow your physician's instructions on administering medication.

Read the warnings and patient advisory information. This material warns you of any possible allergic reactions to medication or other possible side effects. It could save your child's life.

All medications should have childproof caps and be kept out of children's reach. Many medications are made to be child friendly. Medications that are in the form of lollipops or other candy, freezer pops, or juice bottles contain a special hazard to children who can not differentiate between regular treats and medication. These and other medications should always be stored in a locked medicine cabinet.

A well-stocked medicine cabinet should contain the following items. (This list is meant to be used as a glossary of available products as well as their uses. I am not, however, advocating or endorsing any specific product to be used in place of professional medical advice.)

Adhesive bandages: Sterile bandages designed to cover and protect wounds.

Allergy medication: Used to treat common indoor and outdoor allergy symptoms, including stuffy nose, runny nose, sneezing, itchy, watery eyes, coughing, etc.

Antibiotic ointment: A first-aid antibiotic used to help prevent infection in minor cuts, scrapes, and burns.

Antihistamine: Used to treat allergic reactions.

Baby Powder: Used to absorb and prevent moisture.

Charcoal: Used to neutralize the ingestion of poison. Use only as directed by a physician or the Poison Control Center.

Cold medication: Used for the treatment of common colds, allergies, and upper respiratory infections. Available in a variety of flavors with a variety of products to treat different symptoms, including stuffy nose, runny nose, sneezing, itchy, watery eyes, coughing, etc.

Cotton balls: Good for a variety of uses including cleaning cracks and crevices as well as cuts and scrapes.

Cotton swabs: Ideal for a multitude of uses. If used to clean ears, stroke swab gently around the outer surface of the ear without entering the ear canal.

Diaper Rash Medication: Used to soothe and heal diaper rash.

Digital thermometer: (or other thermometer): For oral, rectal, or underarm use; fast and easy to read temperature.

Fever reduction medication and pain reliever: Helps reduce fever and provide relief of minor aches and pains due to colds, flu, sore throat, headache, and toothache.

Gas Medication: Used to relieve the discomfort of gas and bloating.

Hydrocortisone cream: For the temporary relief of itching due to minor skin irritations, inflammations and rashes due to eczema, insect bites, poison ivy, soaps, detergents, and more. For external use only.

Hydrogen peroxide: A topical antiseptic used to clean wounds and help prevent infection.

Lotion: To prevent drying and chapping and to moisturize dry skin.

Medicine dropper: Used to administer any liquid medicine by mouth as recommended by your child's doctor.

Nasal aspirator: Provides gentle suction to remove excess mucus when your child has a stuffy nose. Helps make breathing easier.

Oral electrolyte maintenance solution: Quickly restores fluid and minerals lost from diarrhea and vomiting. Used to prevent dehydration.

Oral pain reliever: Relieves teething pain, and provides temporary relief of sore gums due to teething.

Petroleum jelly: Helps prevent diaper rash, soothes chapped lips and skin, moisturizes, and lubricates.

Poison reduction medication: To be used after ingestion of a poisonous substance to induce vomiting. (Contact Poison Control before administering.)

Rubbing alcohol or alcohol swabs: An antiseptic skin cleanser. Can be used for cleaning thermometers, tweezers, etc.

Saline nasal spray: Nonmedicated moisturizing nose drops for relief of dry, irritated, stuffy noses due to colds, allergies, dry air (humidity), or air pollution.

Sunscreen: Used to protect skin against the sun's ultraviolet rays, which cause sunburns as well as skin cancer. Fair-skinned internationally adopted children from Eastern Europe may be particularly susceptible to sunburn, as they may have spent little time outdoors and aren't used to the different climate. Use a sun block with an SPF 20 or more and limit the amount of time the child spends in direct sun.

Suppositories: (For babies) Used to treat constipation.

Toddler ice pack: A small ice pack designed to fit a few ice cubes or a freezer ball. Sometimes animal shaped. Used more for moral support for minor bumps or falls than to treat real injuries.

Vaporizing cold medicine: An external medication used through inhalation to provide temporary relief of nasal congestion and coughing due to colds. Also provides relief as a decongestant and cough suppressant.

Chapter 14

The Pediatrician

Selecting A Pediatrician

Choosing a pediatrician is an important step in your child's healthcare plan. A pediatrician will be your child's primary physician. If your daughter has special needs, your pediatrician may have to coordinate a health-care plan or refer you to a specialist, depending on your daughter's needs and your insurance plan.

Because a physician should examine your child soon after his arrival, you should select a pediatrician in advance. The best place to get a physician referral is from parents of young children. Your adoption agency or social worker may know of a physician in the area who has adopted patients. Ask members of any adoption group or other adoptive families in your area whom they recommend. Your obstetrician/gynecologist or primary care physician could also give you physician referrals.

In our case, I was referred to a popular children's clinic. The administrator I spoke to was very insistent that I attend an orientation meeting for new parents instead of scheduling a private consultation. I suspected and, after asking enough questions, confirmed that this orientation meeting was for expectant parents and covered what to expect at the hospital before and after birth and infant care—what to expect during the first few weeks. This was completely inappropriate for a parent who is adopting a fifteen-month-old toddler with specific health concerns and questions, not to mention extremely insensitive to infertility issues of adoptive parents. Furthermore, since I had been clear in my explanation that we would be first-time parents who were adopting a toddler from Eastern Europe, this attitude made me question their ideas and opinions on adoption.

The pediatrician I initially called to set up a consultation never called me back. When I called a second time to schedule a consultation, I was referred to another doctor in this practice. She did not return my call on a timely basis (within two or three days) either. I concluded that since my phone calls were not being returned now; they probably would not be returned when I had other medical questions or emergencies.

In the interim, a friend referred me to another pediatrician. She pointed out that the two practices I had originally been referred to were a twenty- to thirty-minute drive from my home. She felt that even though I make that drive regularly, it might be farther than I would want to drive with a sick child.

The pediatrician my friend Betsy suggested was great. His office was less than ten minutes from my house. He seemed genuinely interested in and supportive of adoption. His parents had visited several orphanages in Eastern Europe, and I assumed that he had a working knowledge of the conditions the children lived in. He also showed a willingness to receive and research medical information pertinent to adoption issues, and he understood what it would mean to have an incomplete medical history and did not consider it a hindrance.

Here are a few things to consider when choosing a pediatrician:

1. What are the office hours?
2. What are the after-hours and weekend policies and procedures?
3. Are there other adopted patients? Are there other patients who are internationally adopted or have the same ethnic background?
4. Does this physician meet your insurance requirements?
5. How long does it take you to drive from your home to the doctor's office?
6. Does the pediatrician have a positive attitude about adoption? Does he or she appear willing to learn more about special needs of adopted children?
7. What is your general impression when you look around the office? Is it neat and clean?
8. Is the staff friendly, courteous, and helpful?

The Consultation

Before your consultation with the pediatrician, you should make a list of the questions that you have. This will help you conduct your interview and remember the important questions. The pediatrician should be willing to review your medical information, be able to discuss your daughter's current medical condition if applicable, and be able to refer you to specialists as necessary. She should be up-to-date on the health issues of internationally adopted children and be willing to seek additional information as recommended by the American Academy of Pediatrics or International Adoption Specialist.

If you have birth children or if it has been many years since you have had a young child in your home, it may be necessary to use a different pediatrician. You might now need one who may be more knowledgeable in adoption issues or one who specializes.

Most pediatricians do not charge for consultations. Out of courtesy, be conscious of the amount of time you spend with the doctor. Make sure your questions have been answered to your satisfaction but do not get off track. This consultation should help you determine whether you would trust this person to oversee your child's health care not teach you child-care basics.

The First Examination

Medical examinations by a pediatrician soon after you reach home are necessary to get an accurate assessment of your daughter's current medical condition. At this time the pediatrician may recommend your daughter see a dentist or pediatric dentist, have an eye exam, or hearing and speech evaluation. He will also address any immediate medical concerns.

See the American Academy of Pediatrics, Provisional Section on Adoption, for medical information on adoption and foster care at *www.aap.org/sections/adoption*. The provisional includes an introduction to the health-care needs of adopted children, the importance of screening tests for internationally adopted children, immunization, and infectious diseases. Some of the most common problems found in children adopted from China are respiratory infections/asthma, intestinal parasites, lead poisoning/exposure, malnutrition/rickets, and developmental delays.

Immunizations

Most medical professionals recognize and consider China's immunization records to be accurate. Even so, you may want to consider re-immunization or testing for antibodies, which will enable your pediatrician to determine if antibodies are low or nonexistent and whether it is necessary to re-immunize. This can be especially important for older children.

Failure to re-immunize and/or failure to check for antigens/antibodies from past immunizations should be a serious red flag and is considered essential for your child's health and safety.

When Do I Call My Pediatrician?

As a new parent, trying to determine whether your child is sick (or sick enough) and whether you should contact the pediatrician can be tricky. When you selected a pediatrician, you should have been given information to help determine if your daughter is sick, if she needs immediate medical assistance, the policies regarding calls received after-hours, and what temperature fever indicates a problem. As with any medical recommendations, always follow the advice of your physician. Reasons to call the pediatrician or other health-care resources may include:

1. Your child looks and acts sick.
2. Your child has a fever of 103 degrees or higher. (Follow *your* pediatrician's recommendation. A lower fever and lethargic child could also warrant a call to the pediatrician. When in doubt, make the call.)
3. Your child has a rapidly rising temperature.
4. Your child will not eat or drink.
5. Your child has dry skin, a dry sticky mouth, no tears, or infrequent wetting. These may be signs of dehydration.
6. Your child vomits after falling or other injury.
7. You are worried about your child's illness.
8. Your child is very sleepy, restless, fussy, or shows other changes in behavior.
9. Your child has had several episodes of diarrhea and/or vomiting.
10. Your child experiences severe diarrhea while on medication.
11. There is blood or mucus in the diarrhea.
12. Your child has difficulty breathing.
13. Your child has a cold that is worsening or accompanied by a fever.
14. Your child is drooling and cannot swallow.
15. You suspect your child may have ingested chemicals, plants, pills, or other hazardous material.

For common illnesses such as a cold or upset tummy, it may not be necessary to consult your pediatrician. Helping ease your daughter's discomfort will be high on your priority list. (The first cold is the worst.) Giving children plenty of fluids and making them rest will help make them feel better.

Make sure your child drinks plenty of fluids. Too much juice can cause diarrhea. Watch for dehydration. Feed your daughter according to her normal schedule. You may need to feed smaller portions and more easily digestible foods such as crackers, mashed potatoes, chicken noodle soup, or toast.

If your daughter has a cold, you may need to use a humidifier in her room to help moisten her breathing passages and sore throat. It may be necessary to prop your child upright in bed to help her breathe more comfortably. A bulb syringe can help clear little noses.

Watch for signs of increased discomfort or an increase or addition of a fever. It is also important never to give a child aspirin. Use an aspirin substitute. Your pediatrician can recommend one.

Changing Pediatricians

Selecting a pediatrician in advance is kind of like shopping for a new dress. It might look good on the rack, but you can't tell how it fits until you try it on. Once your pediatrician actually exams your daughter, you may decide that you do not wish him to continue as her pediatrician.

I "fired" the pediatrician I had selected in advance when the specialist he referred me to because of a positive TB test had to use a medical instrument to remove my daughter's ear wax buildup. I am sure that I had seen the pediatrician check her ears, and this should have been a standard part of any thorough medical exam.

Apparently the pediatrician decided that he was smarter than (or had never read) the information that I had given him containing recommendations by the American Academy of Pediatrics for internationally adopted children. I discussed this with him during our initial consultation and hand-delivered a copy of the report to his office immediately before we traveled.

Instead he refused to test her stool and urine. (Yes, I actually brought samples to the office.) He also refused to run an antibody/antigen test to make sure she had received her immunizations and that what she had received had done its job. He even misquoted the article concerning re-immunization and stated that it was not necessary.

At the time we had been home less than forty-eight hours. I was too tired to argue with him and could not tell him where this information had come from when I tried to question his decision.

This was the same pediatrician who in my interview was very positive about adopted children. He also appeared willing to learn more about their health needs. He also had some knowledge of children in orphanages, as his parents had visited several. I thought this doctor should have been up-to-date on current medical information.

It is amazing that he actually tested for tuberculosis. After a positive TB test, we were referred to a specialist for children's infectious diseases. The specialist was up-to-date on medical concerns for internationally adopted children and knew what should be done. She did everything the pediatrician failed to do.

The stool sample showed that Callie tested positive for giardia and had to be treated. The specialist ran blood tests and even checked her for chickenpox scars. She did not think Callie had been exposed to chickenpox or had immunity. The antibody test showed that she had. Failing to re-immunize or to conduct diagnostic testing could unknowingly leave your child vulnerable to such illness.

Fortunately we went to see her the first week we were home. She also referred me to another wonderful pediatrician. Always have a backup plan. Educate yourself on adoption-related health concerns, and if in doubt, get a second opinion.

Chapter 15

Medical Considerations for Adopted Children

Medical reports for our children are sometimes the largest hurdle that a parent has to face when considering adoption. For children who are abandoned, there is rarely any family history. Historically speaking, medical records for children from China are fairly accurate. However on rare occasions the reports can be incomplete or incorrectly translated. They may need more follow-up, a physician's review of the available information, further research on medical conditions, insurance coverage, and medical resources within your community.

You should never allow yourself to be rushed by an agency to make a decision. You should be given ample time to review a child's medical info, have it evaluated by medical personnel if necessary, and decide whether you would like to accept a referral.

Physicians Who Evaluate Medical Information

More serious or chronic medical conditions should have been diagnosed before a child is available for adoption. The younger a child, the harder it may be to get an accurate diagnosis of certain medical conditions such as Fetal Alcohol Syndrome (extremely rare in China) or Autism. One advantage in adopting older infants or toddlers is that I believe you can get a more accurate diagnosis of a child's medical condition, developmental level, general personality, and well being.

There are physicians who are experienced in and available to evaluate medical information and videotapes (not usually available from China) of children. Physicians who review medical information of internationally

adopted children are experienced in evaluating children who were premature, had low birth weight, or have developmental delays as a result of being
institutionalized from birth. If the evaluation results in a negative prognosis or
a possible medical condition, consider a second opinion.

If two physicians independently arrive at the same or similar conclusions,
that helps eliminate the likelihood of misdiagnosed medical conditions.
However, a physician's review of videotapes or medical data can never replace
a physical examination. Some medical conditions have no physical symptoms.
Without a physical examination, it is possible for a physician to misdiagnosis a
medical condition or suspect one that the child does not actually have.

Doctors are more likely to err on the side of caution. If a physician suspects
a child has a medical condition, he or she should be able to give you specific
details, an explanation, and the reason for his suspicions. The doctor has an
obligation to the family who may have already, at least on some level, bonded
with this child to help them understand the risk factors and what they should
consider acceptable risks.

Medical Records

Medical history for adopted children may be inaccurate, incomplete, or nonexistent. Be aggressive; insist on obtaining as much medical information as
possible about your child's current medical condition, living arrangements,
or developmental history. Once an adoption is complete, it may be virtually
impossible to obtain any additional information.

One of the most common complaints among adoptive parents is a misdiagnosed medical condition. This can occur for a variety of reasons. Most
commonly, medical terminology is used differently in other countries or a
broad-based term may be used to describe a possible medical condition. *Note:
this is much more common in Eastern European adoptions.

Incomplete medical information may occur due to record keeping, a
frequent change in caregivers or social workers, or simply a lack of background
information or history.

It is also possible that medical information may not actually be missing
because there was in fact no medical care available. Children who are available
for adoption in China rarely have any birth parent information. On occasion
notes for or about babies along with birth dates can be found with them.
Children who are in orphanages may be located in remote regions where it is
difficult to get information in and out or there may be laws that set limitations
on the type and amount of information that is disclosed.

We were given copies of our daughter's medical records and had them translated by the facilitating agency. There were still gaps, what we were given was a summary not a literal translation. You may wish to have papers like this translated by a third party, preferably someone who is a physician or at least familiar with medical terminology in your child's native country.

In the back of my Blue Cross/Blue Shield physician-listing booklet, I found a section of physicians who are bilingual. While my daughter's pediatricians are two Asian women, I found a Russian-speaking pediatrician in the next city.

Children in Orphanages

"Orphanages, regardless of quality of care, are not good places for children. Orphanage care, or essentially lack of care, can result in a variety of developmental delays. The good news is that children are extremely resilient and can overcome many of their obstacles. However, adopting an older infant, toddler, or older child is not the same as adopting a new born or young infant and each will come with there own unique circumstances."

It is not uncommon for children who are living in orphanages or other less-than-desirable living conditions to have vitamin deficiencies, anemia, impetigo, lactose intolerance, failure to thrive, internal parasites, tooth decay, lice or other medical conditions that may need immediate attention. You may need to consider taking a variety of medications with you when you travel to adopt your child. (See Chapter 18, "Packing for Your Trip.")

While incidences in children adopted from China are reportedly much lower, than those adopted from many other countries, behavioral or medical conditions for children who have resided in orphanages or experienced frequent changes in caregivers may include sensory deprivation and integration, attention deficit disorders, learning disabilities, and attachment disorders.

Adopted children, regardless of country of origin, are at risk for attachment issues. (Even non-adopted children can be diagnosed with Reactive Attachment Disorder) *Every* adoptive parent needs to include research and seek out resources on bonding and attachment as a part of their pre-adoption education.

For more information on Reactive Attachment Disorder and Post traumatic Stress Disorder in Chinese children see Attach-China/International at www.Attach-China.org

What may appear to be developmental delays caused by the orphanage environment may be societal rather than environmental and common in certain cultures. One example of commonly seen in Chinese children is the practice of bundling or swaddling of babies. While this can lead to developmental delays in gross and fine motor skills, by US standards, this is common in many children in China whether they reside in an orphanage or not.

The children may also have been premature, had low birth weight, or rarely prenatal exposure to drugs, nicotine, and alcohol. Frequent ear infections and possible hearing loss as a result of infection are also not uncommon in orphanage babies who are left unattended with their bottles. The quality of the water, a lack of fluoride, and poor hygiene can lead to tooth decay and gum disease. Children with lactose intolerance may show symptoms as infants with this condition becoming more prevalent as the child gets older. Asian children may be more likely to develop this condition.

Chronic medical disorders should have been disclosed prior to your decision to adopt your child. These may include hepatitis B or C, tuberculosis, and congenital heart disease. Congenital disorders could include cleft palate and cleft lip. Neurodevelopmental disorders include Down syndrome, fetal alcohol syndrome, fetal alcohol effect, and cerebral palsy. HIV and AIDS are on the increase in developing countries.

Some of the most common medical diagnosis for children adopted from China are, malnutrition, (the most common cause of growth failure) rickets, poor dental hygiene, skin conditions such as eczema and scabies, asthma, and lead poisoning.

I have not gone into detail, as much of this information is already available through other adoption and medical-related media. One of the best medical resources for health issues in Chinese children is Dr Jane Aronson's web-site www.orphandoctor.com. You may also find additional reference material in the Resource section in the back of this book.

Love Marks and Mongolian Spots

Two commonly mistaken birthmarks are known as love marks and Mongolian spots. Love marks possibly seen in children adopted from China are small scars, usually on the stomach or chest. These scars resemble a small burn but are actually made with acupuncture needles or a lighted medicinal plant. This ancient practice is a way of letting the child know that their birth parents loved them and should be considered an important part of their heritage.

Mongolian spots are spots that look like bruises but are in fact birthmarks common in children of Asian or Indian decent. These black-and-blue marks are usually on the lower back and buttocks and are sometimes mistaken for bruises. As the child gets older, these marks usually fade but may not completely disappear.

Bransen, who is adopted from Vietnam, has them and even though I knew what Mongolian spots were, had his mother not shown me, I would not have recognized them when I saw them. They looked like ink stains, and his mother told me that a nurse at the doctor's office had mistaken them for that.

If your child has Mongolian spots or love marks, you will need to inform and educate caregivers, babysitters, teachers, or medical personnel ahead of time. It may be necessary to show them and you should have your pediatrician document them in your child's medical records with specific references as soon as possible. You may want to include pictures of them in her medical records. This may save you and your child's caregivers possible embarrassment if they inadvertently see them and think the worst.

Medical Support and Available Resources

If you are adopting a special needs child or have adopted a child who is discovered to have physical, cognitive, developmental or speech and language problems you should find out what resources are available in your area. Your adoption agency, social worker, or home study coordinator may be able refer you to state and federally mandated programs, including rehabilitation and subsidies. Other resources include your pediatrician, social services, local children's hospitals, specialized support groups, adoption support groups, international/ethnic organizations, the Internet, your insurance company, the school system, or other children's agencies.

As a precaution, consider finding a family counselor or child therapist in case you need help during your adjustment period or if you have bonding issues or concerns.

If your child is a toddler or older child, it may be necessary to secure an interpreter prior to placement. Our daughter was three when we adopted her. My cousin's wife is Russian and was able to serve as an interpreter. Another couple who adopted an older child had an interpreter visit regularly so they were able to communicate better with their daughter while she learned English. This could be potentially life-saving in case of illness or an emergency.

Callie was born with a cleft lip and palate. I was able to contact our pediatrician and get several physician referrals including a plastic surgeon, children's hospital, and a genetics center. Each referral was able to give me more referrals. While researching Callie's medical condition, I was able to find resource information on the Internet from the Cleft Palate Foundation, various support groups, and a variety of specialists.

We were able to assess her current medical condition, learn what medical procedures might be necessary, and her prognosis. We were also able to see before-and-after pictures of children with similar medical conditions, get cost estimates, and check insurance coverage. We also were also able to select two cleft teams who would evaluate our daughter upon her arrival.

If your daughter has a known medical problem, you have an obligation to yourself and your child to make informed decisions concerning her medical treatment. You must be mentally and physically prepared and financially able to provide the best treatment possible. Know your options.

Child Development

Speech and language delays are one of the most common types of developmental delays and a good indicator of other possible developmental issues. How well your daughter can speak and understand will depend on how much she is talked and listened to. Generally speaking the better a child is speaking at the time of adoption, the faster they will learn their new language. Most adoptive parents only learn some of the most basic words and phrases. While this may come in handy for toddlers or older children the majority of children adopted from China are 18 months of age and younger.

The wait ands see approach commonly used by speech and language therapist is not appropriate for internationally adopted children who are already language delayed. To do so can actually increase or worsen the delay.

The following guidelines by age may be a useful tool in accessing and monitoring language development:

Age 9 months

> Copies speech sounds
>
> Stops when told no
>
> Reponses to name
>
> Changes vocal pitch
>
> Responds differently to different tones of voice, (cheerful or angry)
>
> Turn towards sound and try to locate it
>
> Reciprocates Smiles
>
> Social Play such as peek-a-boo

Age 12 Months

Uses 1 word correctly

Acknowledges loud sound by waking up or by other movement

Looks towards sound

Hands you item requested

Responds to music

Uses simple gestures

Imitates actions

Age 12-15 Months

Learns to find and point to body parts

Dance to music

Learn or know animal sounds

Like to look at books

Age 15-18 Months

Points to known objects when asked

Use 3-4 words correctly

Copy tones of voice

May like objects that make noise

Repeats name of object he wants

Start to like hide and seek

Pretend play

Age 18-21 Months

Ask for objects she wants by name

Match object to sound

Point to pictures she knows by name

Likes to "help" doing chores

Likes to play ball

Wants to count in hide and seek

Age 21-24 Months

    Follows simple instructions

    Knows 3-5 body parts by name

    Uses words and made up words when talking

    Talks on toy telephone

    Clap, march, sing, and use musical instruments

    Can answer sounds that animals make

    Uses 2-4 word phrases

    Interested in other children

Age 2 to 3 Years

    Use words to tell or ask for something

    Uses own name

    2-3 word sentences

    Interested in TV or radio

    Enjoys playing in water

    Glue pictures on paper

    Help mix cookie dough

    Shows affection for playmates

Age 3 to 4 Years

    Speaks intelligibly—most people can understand her most of the time

    4 word sentences

    Knows approximately 900 words

    Has favorite books

    Talks about story/pictures in books

    Uses crayons

    Uses blunt scissors and paper

    Enjoys playing with other children

    Plays make believe

Ages 4-5 Years

> Can tell you about specific events
>
> Knows 1500 words
>
> Enjoys more complex books
>
> Watches age appropriate TV
>
> Participates in family conversation
>
> Follows 2-3 step commands
>
> Cooperates with other children

By age five, children should know what objects are and what they are made of. They should understand opposites: up-down, in front of and behind. By age five the vocabulary should be approximately 2000 words and speak in five to six word sentences. Children should be able to tell a story well and talk about feelings, wishes, fears, etc. When talking children should make most speech sounds correctly and use real words not baby talk.

Hearing Loss

In order to speak correctly you must be able to hear properly. Small hearing loss can be contributed to frequent ear infections. Ear infections are common in children adopted from China. Children with cleft lip/palates may not hear properly until after the cleft palate is repaired. This can negatively affect language as well as speech, especially in older toddlers and young children. Hearing loss can occur at anytime. The good news is that hearing can be tested at any age. Signs of hearing loss are:

Age 0-6 Months

> No response to loud noise

Age 6-12 Months

> Does not look for sounds
>
> Reaction to sound is inconsistent
>
> Does not babble or there is a decrease in babble

Age 12 Months or Older

>Does not respond when called

>Ask a lot of questions

>Wants music or TV to loud

>Starts talking less

>Frequent ear infections—at any age

Identifying Learning Difficulties

If you suspect that your daughter has learning difficulties, it is important to remember that proper diagnosis and intervention are the key to her educational success. Indicators of learning issues which may merit further investigation are:

>General Developmental delays—walking, talking late

>Trouble understanding directions

>Trouble following directions in sequence

>No interest in reading, or other learning activities

>Difficulty with learning letters (or writing)

>Difficulty with spelling

>Trouble with reading comprehension

>Difficulty with rhymes

>Problems organizing thoughts

>Slow to learn new skills

>Problems with homework

>Does not like school

>Child says she is dumb

>Behavior problems in school

>Confusion with handedness (no dominant hand preference-by age five)

>Problems with learning retention or memory recall

>Poor concentration or attention span

>Immature behavior

>Self-regulation issues

Developmental Assessment, Early Intervention Programs, and Speech Therapy

An examination to determine your daughter's developmental level is essential for adopted children. If your daughter has been in an orphanage, he will probably be developmentally behind, at the rate of approximately one month behind for every three to four months in the orphanage.

This should help qualify most adopted children for some type of services, whether it is speech, occupational, or physical therapy. If your daughter is under age three, contact a local early intervention program that can assess her need for special education or related services.

Once your daughter's developmental level has been determined, consider enrolling her in activities that are at her developmental level rather than at her actual age. This may involve advocating for the rights of your child.

Sometimes programs are subject to individual interpretation of the laws or rules regarding eligibility. Occasionally there is prejudice against internationally adopted children. It may be necessary to contact your local congressional representative, senator, or other government official to ensure that your daughter receives the benefits that she is entitled to.

It pays to know the actual terms of eligibility for state and federal programs. The Individuals with Disabilities Education Act states, "All children with disabilities must be provided free and appropriate education." Programs for children over three are usually overseen by the school district, and they are required to test in the child's native language. If your daughter is age three or older, do not wait until your child understands English before testing for eligibility for services.

The trick is getting an appointment before your child loses her native language and does not have enough of her adopted one. Most developmental tests for children who are toddler and preschool age are language based and should be conducted by a speech and language pathologist not a psychologist.

If a child is developmentally delayed, she may be considered learning disabled based on test scores, even if she is simply a year behind. A developmental delay, regardless of the reason, is considered a disability. However, she may only participate in age-appropriate programs, not developmentally appropriate public programs, including preschool and kindergarten.

The reason for this is simple: money. State or federally funded programs receive their money on a per-student basis, and the criterion is chronological age. I strongly disagree with this practice. Adopted children should be eligible for developmentally appropriate, not age-appropriate, therapy and education.

Most public early intervention programs and child development programs are either fully or partially funded by state or federal funds. There is often a delay in getting appointments, completing the assessments, and beginning services. Much of this is due to the meeting the eligibility requirements to begin a program and completing the paperwork. If this sounds vaguely familiar, that's because it is. Apparently these offices work with the same sense of urgency that many offices we are already familiar with do when processing adoption paperwork.

If your child is eligible for services, an Individual Education Plan (IEP) will be developed, and it will be necessary to research your child's disability and know your rights. At times, it may be necessary to enlist the aid of an advocacy group. What you consider to be appropriate services for your child may not coincide with your school district's idea of appropriate. For example, placing a speech-delayed child in a classroom with hearing-impaired children or with children who are learning disabled because they are a year behind age-appropriate peers.

Because our daughter had a cleft lip/palate, she was eligible to receive speech therapy. During this assessment, she had a developmental assessment and was required to have a speech and hearing assessment as well as a vision check. Speech therapy is a federally mandated program. All children over the age of three are eligible for free speech services.

I was told that because of Callie's cleft, she was immediately eligible to begin speech therapy; normally children who are learning English as a second language are required to wait two years before they can enter a program. For a toddler who is not speaking but should be, two years is two years to late to begin speech therapy. If all else fails consider private speech therapy.

Many school systems offer classes in English as a second language (ESL). These classes usually start at age four, and many children in these classes speak Spanish as their first language. Many internationally adopted children have language delays in their native tongue, so it is not simply a matter of ESL. This program works on the concept that your language development is age appropriate, however language delays experienced by internationally adopted children would make ESL inappropriate for them.

Plan ahead. I waited until after our daughter had recovered from her palate repair surgery to set the initial appointment for an evaluation to begin speech therapy. The appointment was set for six weeks after I called. In total, it took us four months before our daughter could begin to receive speech therapy. Of course as my frustration began to increase, I was told if I did not like it to call my congressional representative. This comment was unnecessary and unwarranted because I had not even begun to get angry at that point. (I should have called)

Since this program is offered through the school program, Callie only received three months of therapy before school was out for the year. She was able to attend a six-week summer program. In total, the first year home, she only received four and a half months of therapy.

It took us four months to get an appointment to see a developmental pediatrician. First, no one responded to our pediatrician's multiple referrals; then they sent us a package of papers to fill out, their office moved, it was Christmas, and finally, they lost our paperwork (luckily I had keep copies). I had no idea that after taking four months to get an appointment, it would take three months to get the assessment.

Misdiagnosis of Medical Conditions

It may be impossible to diagnose some medical conditions before your daughter arrives home and is examined by the pediatrician. Most experts recommend that a pediatrician examine your child within twenty-four to forty-eight hours of arrival. This examination should be a basic "everything looks okay; let's address any immediate concerns, and let's schedule a more thorough examination in a few weeks after your daughter gets more adjusted."

The good news is that with proper diet, nutrition, and medical care, many children have a remarkable growth and development spurt within their first year home. Asian children will be genetically pre-disposed to be smaller than their U.S. peers. Children in North China are larger than their Southern peers. You can locate a growth chart for Chinese children at htpp://www.fwcc.org/growthchart.html. You may wish to print a copy of this and take with you to the pediatricians office.

Medical conditions for internationally adopted children may sometimes be overlooked or misdiagnosed because their conditions may be less common in the United States. Diseases and illnesses that are common overseas may be very rare or even nonexistent in the United States. Adopted children could also be at higher risk for contracting an illness that children born in the United States either have some natural immunities from or were immunized for.

If in doubt of your child's medical diagnosis, or if medication is not working, be persistent. You are your child's health-care advocate. Use your adoption networking resources. Chances are you are not the first person who has experienced this.

Chapter 16

Child-care, Preschool, and Babysitters

One of the most controversial issues of all time is child-care. While religion and politics are always two hotly contested subjects, you will soon learn that there is one more: being a stay-at-home mom versus being a mom who works outside the home. Neither side gets its much-deserved respect.

I can still remember a former employer contemptuously spitting out the words, "She doesn't have a clue. The biggest decision she will make today is what is for dinner." While this attitude can be found in the work place, there is sometimes resentment from childless coworkers who can't appreciate the need for time off to care for a sick child, new baby, etc. Although it certainly does not hold true for everyone, I have found that many employees secretly long to be a stay-at-home parent.

Even those who should know what staying at home entails (like friends, husbands and fathers) are often clueless. I was responsible for purchases in excess of $10 million and regularly worked 60-plus-hour weeks. As a stay-home mom, I worked in excess of 100 hours a week and did not get to go home at the end of the day and rest and unwind. I worked at home from morning to night. The job is never-ending and far from glamorous. When people asked what I did all day, I tell them I ate bonbons and watched soap operas. It didn't matter if they believed me or not, it's what they thought.

Whether you have the luxury of staying at home or must make sacrifices to stay at home with your child, or you choose to work or must continue working, you will still need to use an occasional babysitter and be responsible for having an educational plan for your child.

Babysitters

On occasion, everyone needs time away from their children, whether it is a night out with friends, a quiet evening alone with your spouse, or time to run errands. Your needs will vary and will be determined by your toddler's age, adjustment, and development.

The best place to find a babysitter is through friends or personal references. Among the best sitters I've found are our friends' children. We always told them that we would have children when theirs were old enough to baby-sit, and that has worked out perfectly. Of course, they do have to vie with Grandma and Grandpa who cherish the opportunity to spend quality time with their grand-children. It is definitely advantageous to have at least one set of grandparents living in the same area.

If using a service or a sitter you are unfamiliar with, always meet the person in advance and check references. Your child's needs will determine what age sitter would be appropriate. The more needs your child has, the more experienced a sitter you need. Sitters should never be under age thirteen, and many cities have child-care/babysitter training available for teens. Your sitter should be respon-sible enough to act accordingly in a minor emergency. Having first aid and/or CPR training is also a big plus.

Ask your sitter to arrive early so you can show her or him around the home, give instructions, answer questions, and review potential problems. Show the sitter where first-aid kits and flashlights are located and give emergency contact numbers. Is there a neighbor he can contact if necessary? Leave emergency numbers, cell phone numbers, beeper numbers, and the location and phone number where you will be by the phone.

Tell the sitter when you will return home and, when applicable, be sure her parents approve the time she will be home. If you are going to be late, inform both the sitter and her parents.

Child-care

Most people would like to enjoy the best of both worlds; that is, working a limited amount of hours doing a job they enjoy, being able to afford a reduction in hours, and having their child in a part-time program with other children. For those who wish to pursue this, it may take some creative thinking by both you and your employer.

You may wish to choose in-home daycare or use a daycare center. Your best resources come from other parents. Ask friends, coworkers, your doctor's office, your social worker, or your adoption agency for suggestions. Child-care sources could include your church, child development centers, newspaper ads, or other child-care agencies, including those that specialize in nannies or au pairs.

If you choose to have in-home care, you may have more decision-making freedom regarding how your child spends her time, what she is fed, the rules regarding discipline, and so on. In-home daycare is often more expensive than a daycare center. When choosing in-home care, use a child-care service or an agency to help you find the best-qualified person to suit your needs.

Consider your options and then screen, select, and check references on sitters or programs that you may be more interested in. Before you interview a sitter or visit a daycare center, decide what is important to you and prepare a list of questions. When trying to determine which program is best for you, consider the following:

- Is the daycare licensed or registered per state requirements? How long has it been in operation?

- What are the caregiver's qualifications? Do they require a degree in child development or other related subjects? How long has your child's caretaker/teacher been employed?

- What are the admissions requirements? Are they reasonable? What other requirements must be met before enrolling your child (such as immunizations, potty training, etc.)?

- Is the location convenient, and do the hours of operation suit your needs?

- Do they charge late fees? What are the costs, and are they reasonable for the services provided? What is the pickup and drop-off policy?

- What is the child to caregiver ratio? (State requirements will vary.) What is the age of children in attendance, are the children grouped by age.

- Do they have an open-door policy? Do they encourage parent participation or observation? Is the staff accessible to parents?

- What are polices involving sick children, accidents, and so on? Do caretakers have training in CPR or first aid? What is the policy regarding emergencies? Do they report all accidents to parents?

- Are the premises neat and clean? Are safety features or other childproofing devices visible? What is the condition of the toys, playground and so?

- Are classrooms dark, small, or sparsely furnished, or are they roomy and cheerful with artwork exhibited? Do children in attendance appear happy or complacent? Do you get good "vibes" or are you hearing warning bells? Do you think your child would enjoy spending time here?
- Do they offer preschool-equivalent educational services, field trips or other activities, or do children have continuous supervised free play?
- How are birthday parties or other holidays celebrated?
- Do children have naps or quiet time? What are the sleeping arrangements? Are there separate areas for sleeping, play, food preparation, and toilet needs? Does the facility provide snacks or meals, and if so are they nutritious?
- Do they provide references? The best are those you get by word-of-mouth from someone you know, not those provided by the center.
- How do they handle child conflict or discipline?
- What is the policy regarding (voluntarily or involuntarily) dropping the program?
- Is it racially diverse? What is the ethnic mix? Are their other adopted children?

Preschool

I relished the fact that my children attended preschool. In theory, that meant I had "me" time. While my free time is important to me, how my children spend their time is equally important.

Once a month I received an itinerary of school activities, which included subjects discussed in class, colors, and numbers, as well as physical activities, music time, and chapel. I enjoyed receiving these because I can ask specific questions about their day or know what they missed if they were not at school.

Preschool is the time for children to learn social skills such as sharing, taking turns, and cooperation. There are a variety of preschool programs available. Some programs will focus more on academic achievements. Many will be provided by faith-based organizations, while others are strictly private institutions or provided through the public school system. While most of the considerations for daycare are the same when choosing a preschool, they should also include the following:

- Does the school focus on an educational curriculum or more on social interaction? Which is more appropriate for your child?
- How long is the class? How many days a week?
- Do they offer extended stay?
- Do they have parent and teacher conferences? How often?
- What type of activities do they do? Arts, crafts, books, music, outdoor play, field trips, etc.?
- What are the program's goals or expectations for your child?
- Do they provide school supplies or do you?

Special Considerations for Adopted Children

Choosing the right daycare or preschool program is never an easy process, especially if you have many options. However, as a parent of an adopted child, you should be aware of some special considerations. Most important, is your child ready to attend daycare or preschool, or have a regular babysitter?

Separation Anxiety and the Fear of Being Left

Most likely, your daughter's classroom will consist of one room with one or two teachers and a lot of children. If that sounds vaguely familiar to you, just think how familiar it will feel to her. She may have a fear of being left or experience separation anxiety. While it can be traumatic, it is not uncommon for children—adopted or not.

Your daughter may be terrified, thinking she is being abandoned or "returned." She may find any unfamiliar area upsetting. This may be the result of previous disruptions, insecure or newly formed attachment, inconsistent care, or grief.

If there is a high employee turnover rate at the daycare center, you may need to reconsider. Consistency is very important for adopted children. How much personal attention will your toddler receive? There should be enough caretakers to hold, cuddle, or comfort her.

Give her time to adjust to her new schedule. You may choose to start slowly, while others jump right in. Say goodbye calmly. If you are distraught, she will sense it. Help engage her in activities. Enlist help from teachers if necessary. Kiss your daughter goodbye and reassure her that you will be returning to get her after work, lunch, naptime, etc. Turn around and leave. Initially do not look back, pop in to "visit" or peep back in. If you are caught you are sunk. It does not make it easier on parents to leave when the last image they have is of their crying baby. Be prepared, it is harder on Mommy than on your child. Never sneak out when your child is not looking; this can create trust issues. After time she will adjust and feel secure in the knowledge that you will be returning.

On the other hand, some children may be totally unaffected by attending daycare or preschool. For a recently adopted child, or one who is secure in her attachment, this may be an easy transition, and she may easily accept this as part of her new routine.

Indifference for children who have been home for some time should be looked at more closely to ensure bonding and attachment are progressing. Sometimes children may become attached to caregivers and may not want to leave or experience confusion when it is time to go home. This is a situation you need to watch closely; you may need to rethink your child-care options.

The Classroom and Curriculum

Prepare in advance. We drove by Callie's preschool quite often before she started attending. Each time we told her this was her new school that she would be going to in the fall. When the first day of school arrived, she was very excited and well prepared.

Learning social skills was Callie's biggest obstacle. In an orphanage, the squeaky wheel gets the grease, and it is not uncommon for workers to have favorites. Callie was a favorite and the only girl in her age group. She did not understand that she was not the teacher's assistant but was supposed to sit with the rest of the children. She also learned it pays to be cute and was a master of diversionary techniques when being scolded.

Preschools usually focus on an educational curriculum or social interaction. You need to decide which is more appropriate for your child: learning cooperation, taking turns, sharing, having increased social interaction in a noncompetitive environment, or focusing on academics, catching up to same-age peers, learning letters or numbers? (These elements do overlap to some extent.)

Programs should stimulate development in a nonstressful environment while not being overly demanding or too advanced. Your child should be comfortable in his classroom setting and not overwhelmed, stressed, or lost.

Consider the length of time in class versus at home. We opted to hold Callie back a year in school, starting 3K not 4K as was age-appropriate. Maturity level, length of time in an orphanage, and significant cleft-related speech delays all played a role in this decision. We also did not feel that we wanted her to spend more time away from home than at home, considering that she was three at the time of her adoption. Even though we had very little issues with bonding and attachment, we felt it was more important to continue strengthening her adjustment to family life.

Special-Needs Children

How does the school feel about children who have not learned to speak, are learning English as a second language, or are developmentally delayed? What are the rules involving conduct or other nonharmful inappropriate behavior? Do they appear positive or apprehensive about adoption? Do they ask inappropriate adoption-related questions? What questions were you asked? Are they genuinely interested in your daughter or are they interested in sensationalism?

You should discuss in detail any concerns or special needs that your child has. The more information that you can provide (excluding personal specifics such as the child was abandoned at a maternity hospital, etc.), the better understanding your daycare provider may have.

Find out if there are other adopted children or if they have experience with dealing with adopted children. If your child has special needs, are they able to accommodate him? What are the procedures regarding special dietary needs or administering medication?

Have a Backup Plan

Once your daughter arrives home, you may decide that your predetermined child-care plan does not suit her needs. In some cases, children need more time with their new families before beginning a child-care program; their medical needs may be greater than anticipated; or a parent may decide to change his or her work schedule. Having a backup plan will help should the need arise.

Chapter 17

International Adoption Travel

In 1990, the total number of immigrant visas issued to orphans coming to the United States was 7,093. In 2000, this total had more than doubled to 17,718. According to the U.S. Department of State's, Office of Children's Issues, in fiscal year 2005 there were 22,728 immigrant visas issued to orphans coming to the United States. This is a 22 percent increase from 2000.

For the first time since 1991, international adoption decreased by almost 1 percent between 2004 and 2005. There were single digit increases between 2001 through 2004. This would suggest that perhaps the number of families adopting internationally has leveled off.

Approximately 40 percent of children were toddlers, one to four years of age. Of the approximate 40% under the age of one, most are six months old and older with an average age of 9-10 months at the time of adoption. This is due to a variety of reasons but most often due to birth country requirements.

In 2005, more than 35% of all internationally adopted children were adopted from China. This is a 5% increase from 2004, or additional 862 children adopted from China. Of these, an estimated 97 percent were girls age 2 and under. Interestingly, their was a decrease of 1226 children adopted from Russia between 2005 and 2004.

For 2005, the top seven countries of adoption by U.S. citizens are as follows:

Country	# of Adoptions
China	7,906
Russia	4,639
Guatemala	3,783

South Korea	1,630
Ukraine	821
Kazakhstan	755
Ethiopia	441

Approximately 88 percent of all international adoptions by U.S. citizens took place in these seven countries.

Traveling Abroad

Before traveling to complete an international adoption, families should review Consular Information Sheets and Travel Warnings. This information is available from the State Department's Bureau of Consular Affairs through the Office of American Services and Crisis Management (ACS). It can be found on the Internet at *http://travel.state.gov/or* by calling (888) 407-4747. 317-472-2328 or (202)-501-4444 from overseas.

Consular information sheets are available for every country in the world. This information may include a description of the country, entrance and exit requirements, HIV testing requirements, areas of instability, aviation safety and air travel, traffic safety and road conditions, medical facilities, crime information, currency exchange, customs regulations, adoption, drug penalties, and registration at U.S. embassy locations.

You may also find listings for services and other pertinent information for citizens who are abroad. These listings include the numbers for emergency services; where to go for help with lost or stolen passports, financial assistance, arrest and incarceration; lists of doctors and hospitals; and links to U.S. embassies and consulate Web sites.

As a safety precaution, always carry consulate and embassy locations, address and phone numbers with you at all times when traveling overseas.

Safety and Security

Security personnel may place foreign visitors under surveillance. Hotel rooms, telephones and fax machines may be monitored. Problems with authorities may occur if you take photographs of anything that could be perceived as being of military or security interest.

China is a safe country with a crime rate that is low but on the increase. Pickpockets may target tourists, especially at sightseeing destinations, open-air markets and in stores. Do not depend upon security guards to act as deterrent's. Visitors should exercise due caution in public areas. You my wish to place valuables in the hotel safe or leave them at home.

Avoid carrying large amounts of cash walking alone and only use licensed taxis. You should have small bills (RMB 10, 20 and 50 notes) for travel by taxi. Reports of taxi drivers using counterfeit notes to make change for large bills are common. Be sure to get a receipt from the taxi driver.

Travelers may be asked to exchange money at a preferential rate. Due to the large volume of counterfeit currency, these unofficial exchanges usually result in travelers losing their money. It is illegal to exchange dollars for RMB except at official exchange offices, at banks, and hotels.

U.S. Passports are extremely valuable on the black market. The loss or theft abroad of your passport should be reported immediately to the local police and the nearest U.S. Embassy or Consulate. Visitors to China should carry their passports with them in a secure location, out of reach of pickpockets. Travelers should make photocopies of their passport and Chinese visas to be kept in a separate, secure location, and to register with the nearest Embassy or Consulate General.

Health Information

You may find that a variety of immunizations are recommended for illnesses not commonly found in the United States are recommended. The Center for Disease Control (CDC) has recommendations for international travelers by country or region at *http://cdc.gov/*or for China information see: *htpp://www.cdc.gov/travel/eastasia/htm.*

The CDC recommends the following vaccines for travelers to China:

- Hepatitis A or immune globulin (IG)
- Hepatitis B, if you might be exposed to blood (Hep B positive child), or be exposed through medical treatment.
- Typhoid, particularly if you are visiting developing regions.
- As needed, booster doses for tetanus-diphtheria and measles.

See your doctor at least 4–6 weeks before your trip to allow time for most shots to take effect. In addition you may need a flu shot, other immunizations or health precautions, depending upon where you will be traveling.

Insurance should cover immunizations, but you may want to check with your health-care provider in advance. If your insurance company is denying coverage, have your physician's office call them and forward the CDC's recommendations and risk of exposure. It may be necessary to appeal if insurance coverage has been denied. It may also be possible to have immunizations done at the health department. They are usually less expensive.

When being tested for HIV testing prior to your adoption, it may be significantly less expensive at the health department.

Travelers' diarrhea, is the number one illness in travelers. The single most important dietary rule is do not drink the water! Use bottled water only. Local water supplies may be contaminated with parasites or other waterborne illnesses that locals are either immune to or have adjusted to. Intestinal parasites can cause severe cramping, diarrhea, nausea, vomiting, dehydration, and weight loss.

Besides not drinking the water, do not use ice, ice products like frozen drinks, or brush your teeth with the tap water. Use caution not to swallow any water while swimming or bathing. Do not wash fresh fruits or vegetables in local water. All fruits and vegetables should be peeled before eaten. Bottled water should be readily available. Some people opt to bring water filtration systems with them, but you may find that the cost and added inconvenience is not worth the weight and inexpensive water filters may only be partially effective.

If you regularly wear a medical ID bracelet, you should continue to do so on your trip to China. You should know and take your blood type, including whether you are RH positive or negative. This is especially important if you are RH negative. Almost all Chinese are RH positive. Because of this, medical personnel would not make this distinction in the unlikely event of a transfusion. This may be a critical care factor if you are in an accident.

Preventative Health Care Recommendations

- Protect yourself from mosquito bites: Travelers to some areas in China may be at risk for malaria. (Especially Guiyang and Guizhou) Malaria is a serious, preventable infection that can be fatal. You may wish to see your health care provider for a prescription, antimalarial drug. At the least take mosquito repellent spray.

- Don't eat or drink dairy products that are un-pasteurized.

- Don't eat un-cooked food or fruits and vegetables unless you have peeled yourself.
- Never eat undercooked ground beef, poultry, raw eggs, or un-pasteurized dairy products. Raw shellfish can be dangerous to persons with liver disease or compromised immune systems.
- Keep feet clean and dry to prevent fungal and parasitic infections. Do not go barefoot.
- Don't eat food from street vendors.
- Don't handle animals (especially monkeys, dogs, cats, birds)
- Don't swim in fresh water. (especially in southeast, east, and Yangtze River valley) Well-chlorinated swimming pools should be okay.
- Always ask doctors and dentists to use sterilized equipment and be prepared to pay for new syringe needles in hospitals or clinics.
- Tuberculosis is epidemic in China. Get tested 3-6 months after your return.
- Air pollution is a significant problem throughout China. Consult your physician prior to travel to consider the health effects of seasonal smog and heavy pollution. especially if you have asthma or are prone to upper respiratory infections. If you have a prescription for an asthma inhaler, take it with you even if you rarely use it.
- If traveling to parts of Tibet, Qinghai, parts of Xinjiang, and western Sichuan remain alert to signs of altitude sickness. Many of these areas are situated at altitudes over 10,000 feet. Travelers in these areas should seek medical advice in advance of travel, and allow time for adjustment to the high altitude.

The CDC and the WHO regularly update their web sites to reflect changes in what is known about Avian Flu (Bird Flu) and Severe Acute Respiratory Syndrome (SARS). They provide the latest in travel guidance. The CDC also provides SARS guidance for U.S. citizens living abroad at http://www.cdc.gov/ncidod/sars/warden_notice.htm.

Your Childs Health

It would not be uncommon to arrive to find that your daughter has some minor medical aliments that need immediate attention. This might include colds, cough, and ear infections or skin infections such as scabies, or eczema or diarrhea or constipation. You may wish to take a copy of a children's medical guide.

If your child becomes sick your facilitator should be able to assist you in locating a physician or hospital. If you have consulted with an International Adoption Specialist or pre-selected a pediatrician prior to your trip, You will want to make arrangements in advance as to how to contact them if you have medical questions. You should determine the best way to contact them: by e-mail or phone. (factor in time difference when calling) Is their someone who is available at all times and should you call the office, cell or emergency numbers?

Medical Facilities in China and Travel Insurance

Western-style medical facilities are available in Beijing, Shanghai, Guangzhou and a few other large cities in China. Many of these hospitals have so-called VIP wards (gaogan bingfang) which service foreigners, have English-speaking staff and feature up-to-date medical technology, and skilled physicians.

Most hospitals in China will not accept medical insurance from the United States. The exception is the following hospitals, Hong Kong Adventist Hospital, Beijing United Family Hospital, Beijing Friendship Hospital, International Medical Center in Beijing, and Peking Union Medical Center. They are on the BlueCross BlueShield's worldwide network providers—overseas network hospitals' list: To confirm before travel, see: http://www.fepblue.org/wasite/wabenefits/wa-benefitsoverseas04.html.

Travelers will be asked to post a deposit prior to hospital admission to cover the expected cost of treatment. Payment by credit cards may be accepted in hospitals in major cities. Even in the VIP wards of major hospitals, patients may encounter difficulty due to cultural or policy differences. This may include limited access to Chinese hospital medical records, laboratory test results, x-rays, etc.

Many professionals in the travel industry recommend travel insurance. The primary function of this insurance is to help offset the cost of emergency medical evacuations or the repatriation of mortal remains. Coverage may include incidental medical expenses, an emergency family reunion, and accidental death or dismemberment. It may also include necessary political evacuation or expulsion from the host country, trip interruption in case of an emergency, or lost baggage.

The U.S. Department of State strongly urges Americans to consult with their medical insurance company prior to traveling abroad to confirm whether their policy applies overseas and whether it will cover emergency expenses such as a medical evacuation.

U.S. medical insurance plans rarely cover medical costs incurred outside the United States unless additional coverage is purchased. U.S. Medicare and Medicaid programs do not provide payment for medical services outside the United States. When consulting with your insurer, verify whether payment will be made to the overseas healthcare provider or if you will be reimbursed later for expenses you incur.

Both travel agents and private companies offer insurance plans that cover health care expenses incurred overseas, including emergency services such as medical evacuations. One company that offers travel insurance for adoptive families is Travel Protectors. ("a company formed by adoptive parents") They specialize in international travel insurance for inter-country adoption and homeland tours. See http://www.travelprotectors.com or call 1-877-515-9055

For more information on providers, specializing in treating foreigners for medical or dental problems is available at http://www.usembassy-china.org.cn/.

Two private emergency medical assistance firms, SOS International, Ltd., and Medex Assistance Corporation, offer medical insurance policies for travelers. Both have staff in China who can assist in the event of a medical emergency.

SOS International, Ltd.

SOS offers international standard family practice services, emergency medical, and dental services and a range of clinical services, provides medical evacuation, and medical escort services in Beijing, Nanjing, Tianjin and Shekou. 24-hour Emergency Alarm Centers are located in Beijing and Shanghai. Each Alarm Center provides 24-hour hotline services to all our global members when they are in China. SOS has an external network of hospitals, airlines and local authorities. Their services also support remote site medical staff, equipment and facilities.

For medical emergencies *anywhere* in mainland China, Americans can call the SOS International, Ltd., 24-hour Alarm Center in Beijing at telephone (86-10) 6462-9100 or 9000 in Shanghai at (86-21) 6295-0099. SOS International Alarm Centers can also be contacted in Hong Kong at telephone (852) 2428-9900 and in the United States at (215) 245-4707.

For a complete list of services, locations, or to purchase health or travel insurance, consult the SOS website at http://www.internationalsos.com or call *(1-800) 523-8930 (8:30 a.m. to 4:30 p.m. Eastern Time, Monday through Friday)* in the U.S.

Beijing Clinic address: Building C, BITIC Leasing Center
No. 1 North Road, Xingfu Sancun, Sanlitun, Chaoyang District, Beijing 100027
Beijing SOS International Clinic,
telephone: (86-10) 6462-9112, Fax (86-10) 6462-9111.

MEDEX Assistance Corporation

Medex members calling with a medical emergency should call Medex-Emergency in China at telephone (86-10) 6595-8510.

871 Poly Plaza
Beijing 100027
Toll Free Number from China to U.S.: 10811-800-527-0218
Email: info@medexassist.com (Baltimore, Maryland)
U.S. telephone: (1-800) 537-2029 or (1-410) 453-6300 (24 hours)
Emergencies (members only): (1-800) 527-0218 or (1-410) 453-6330
Web site: http://www.medexassist.com/

Heathrow Air Ambulance

Heathrow is an air evacuation service with offices in the United States and England. Travelers can pre-arrange air evacuation insurance and other emergency travel assistance. This service also has a business plan to assist foreigners who lack travel insurance.

Heathrow Air Ambulance Service,
15554 FM, Suite 195 Houston, TX. 77095-2704.
Office telephone 1-800-513-5192.
Office fax 1-832-934-2395.
E-mail: info@heathrowairambulance.com

Medical Facilities in China

Beijing United Family Hospital and Clinics ("BJU")

The only foreign-invested full service international standard 50 bed hospital operating in Beijing, China. Offers a full range of specialties including Family Practice, Internal Medicine, Surgery, Gynecology, Pediatrics, Dentistry, and 24 hour Emergency. Staff is fluent in English, French, German, and Spanish to name a few. This facility accepts credit cards.

#2 Jiang Tai Lu, Chaoyang District, Beijing 100016
(8610) 6433-3960 Fax: (8610) 6433-3963
Emergency Hotline: (8610) 6433-2345
Website: www.bjunited.com.cn

Bayley & Jackson Beijing Medical Center
#7 Ritan Dong Lu, Chaoyang District, Beijing 100020
(8610) 8562-9998 Fax: (8610) 8562-3497
Website: www.bjhealthcare.com

Beijing United Family Clinic—Shunyi
Pinnacle Plaza, Unit # 818, Tian Zhu Real Estate Development Zone
Shunyi District, 101312
(8610) 8046-5432 Fax: (8610) 8046-4383

Peking Union Medical Hospital
1 Shui Fu Yuan, Dong Cheng District, Beijing 100730
Tel: 010-6529-6114 or 010-6529-7292; 24-hours 010-6529-5284
Modern Facilities with English speaking staff. Separate ward for foreign patients.

World Link Shanghai Clinic
Expatriate doctors and imported vaccines.
Shanghai Center #203 W, 1376 Nanjing Xi Lu, 200040
Telephone: 6279-7688. For appointments: 6279-8678
Fax: 6279-7698

Hong Qiao Clinic:
Mandarin City Unit 30, 788 Hong Xu Lu, 201103
Tel: 6405-5788; Fax: 6405-3587

Shanghai United Family Hospital and Clinics
1111 Xian Xia Xi Lu, Chang Ning District, Shanghai 200336 PRC
Website: http://www.shanghaiunited.com/

GlobalDoctor, Ltd., has opened clinics staffed by English-speaking doctors within the VIP wards of government-run hospitals in Chengdu, Nanjing, and Beijing. GlobalDoctor Can be reached by telephone from China at 86-10-8456-9191 or on the Internet at http://www.eglobaldoctor.com/

Document Checklist

You will need to bring the following doucments with you when you travel to China. Because documents and procedures may change, consult with your agency to obtain the most current list.

Adoptive family package from the US Embassy, includes the following:

- I-600
- I-604
- DS-230
- Medical exam
- CCAA referral Acceptance Letter (copy)
- Dossier-1 complete copy including copies of authentifications
- DS-1981 Vaccination Affidavit-must be signed and notarized in the US, use child's Chinese name
- Passport with Visa Stamps
- Passport copies (5 copies of each parents)
- Passport Pictures (2, each spouse)
- Travel Approval (2 originals, 4 copies)
- USCIS Approval letter, I-171H or I-797C (1 copy)
- Visa (5 copies of parents Chinese Visa)

If only one parent is traveling, you will also need the following:

- Employment Letter—signed and notarized shortly before travel
- Federal Tax returns—Complete copies of the 3 most recent years, including schedule and attachments
- Power of Attorney—5 originals, 1 original signed, notarized and authenticated
- 1-600 Form, signed by non-traveling spouse, must be notarized in the US
- I-864/I-864A

Passports

You and anyone traveling to China must have a passport. The Passport can not be within in six months of expiration. If it is, you will have to renew prior to your trip, as the consulate will not issue you a Visa to travel. Make sure that you have several full pages available in your passport for your Chinese Visa. All Passports must be signed by the passport holder with the exception of children under the age of ten.

Customs

Chinese customs authorities may enforce strict regulations concerning temporary importation into or export from China of items such as antiquities or banned publications, including those that may be religious in nature. Chinese authorities have seized documents, literature, or anything that consider to por-nographic, political in nature, or intended for purposes of religious evangelism. Persons seeking to enter China with religious materials in a quantity deemed to be greater than that needed for personal use may be detained fined or expelled. In addition customs authorities may seize books, movies, tapes, and compact disks to determine if they violate Chinese prohibitions.

Counterfeit and pirated goods may be available and illegal. Bringing them back to the United States may result in forfeitures or fines. Information on customs regulations can be found at http://www.ustr.gov.

When you enter China you may need to declare the cash and valuables that you are taking in with you. Flight attendants should have customs forms and should be able to answer questions that you may have. If you make a customs declaration, make sure you have your paperwork stamped as you enter customs and do not lose it because you'll need it when you exit the country.

You should declare all money that you are carrying with you; depending on the amount, it may be necessary for you and your spouse or companion to split the money. It is possible that the customs agent may want to count your money. You should consider this when "hiding" money in multiple locations.

When you return home, it will be helpful if you have made a list of all the souvenirs and items purchased in China and the cost of each. Do not include items such as food, donations, gifts, etc. that you are not taking home with you. Attach this to your customs declaration. You are allowed $800.00 per person of duty free merchandise. Unless you spent more than that, you should not have to pay duty. Items such as artwork, sealed packages of consumable items such as tea, and antiques are not subject to duty. For those who are big spenders the duty is typically 10% of purchase amount. Once you have spent over a certain amount, the duty for large ticketed items such as rugs or fine jewelry, may depend on the item. For more information on paying duty, see U.S. Customs regulations at http://www.cbp.gov/xp/cgov/travel/vacation/kbyg/.

The U.S. Embassy

Before travel to China, adoptive parents should register at the Consular Section, American Citizens Services Section of the American Embassy in China or Consulate General. This will allow the embassy to locate you in case of an emergency, provide updated travel or security advisories, or to provide other information about China including changes on adoption procedures, lists of physicians, attorneys, interpreters and translators.

During your adoption journey, you will be required to visit the U.S. embassy in Guangzhou. You must take your daughter to an interview so that she can be issued a visa to enter the United States. The Embassy is closed on both U.S. and Chinese holidays. The U.S. Embassy in Guangzhou is located at

The U.S. Consulate General in Guangzhou—
http://guangzhou.usembassy-china.org.cn/

This consular district includes the following provinces/regions of China: Guangdong, Guangxi, Hainan, and Fujian.

U.S. Citizen Services
5th Floor
Tian Yu Garden (II phase)
136-142 Lin He Zhong Lu
Tian He District, Guangzhou
Tel: 011-86-20-8121-8000
Fax: 011-86-20-3884-4420
E-mail address is GuangzhouA@state.gov or GuangzhouACS@state.gov for emergencies during normal business hours

Mailing address
Number 1 South Shamian Street,
Shamian Island 200S1 Guangzhou 510133

Emergency Services

If you have an emergency during office hours, call the Consulate at 011-86-20-8158-7605. Emergencies include medical problems, arrests and deaths relating to American Citizens. After-hours emergency assistance may be obtained by calling 011-86-20-8121-6077.

Prior to your exit interview, your child must have had a medical exam either at an American medical clinic or by a physician approved by the embassy. This is usually a brief formality which only assures parents that yes your child appears reasonably healthy. The examination includes the taking of measurements: height, weight, heartbeat, etc. The most convenient site for medical examinations is in Guangzhou at the Guangzhou Health and Quarantine Service, located at 33 Shamian North Road. Telephone: 020-8188-9513.

After your daughter has had her medical examination, either you or your guide will take her documents to the U.S. Embassy. As you enter the U.S embassy, you will be required to go through a security checkpoint. Your guide/translator may or may not be able to enter with you. He should have organized your paperwork for you and explained what you need and what to expect.

On the same day or next you will go back to the embassy for an interview and will receive your daughter's passport and Visa. Interviews may consist of a brief review of the paperwork. and may be done as a group. Paperwork errors or delays can happen and could result in your having to stay a few extra days while they are resolved. There will be many other adoptive families at the embassy, and you will find that some of these families will be on your return flight home.

Documents you need to bring with you to the U.S. Consulate: For your daughter's visa application:

Child's People's Republic of China passport and exit permit
Birth Certificate
Abandonment Certificate
Adoption Registration (Original and translated copy)
Child's passport
Copy of child's and parents passports
Proof of medical examination
Two 1 ¾ inch color visa photos
Form I-864, affidavit of support from the prospective adoptive parent(s) and supporting documentation (Only if both parents are not traveling)
The Chinese notarized documentation
I600 form
Vaccination affidavit

When you receive your daughter's Visa you will also be given a sealed package of Visa papers that should be packed in your carry-on luggage where you can easily reach it. DO NOT open the Visa packet. Packets which have been tampered with could result in being denied entry into the U.S. and require a return trip to China. You will need the Visa packet for immigration when you enter the United States. You will also need to show certain documentation including your daughter's Visa when you leave China. Your agency representative will help you with these requirements. Always review documents for correct name, address, etc.

Other U.S. Embassies and Consulates

U.S. Embassy in Beijing

The Embassy consular district includes the following provinces/regions of China: Beijing, Tianjin, Shandong, Shanxi, Inner Mongolia, Ningxia, Shaanxi, Qinghai, Xinjiang, Hebei, Henan, Hubei, Hunan, and Jiangxi.

> American Citizen Services American Citizen Services
> 2 Xiu Shui Dong Jie PSC 461, Box 50
> Beijing 100600 PRC FPO AP 96521-0002
> Tel: 86-10-6532-3831 ext. 229, after-hours: (86-10) 6532-1910 or
>   010-6532-3831
> Fax: 86-10-6532-4153
> Web-site http://www.usembassy-china.org.cn/
> E-mail address is AmCitBeijing@state.gov

The U.S. Consulate General in Chengdu

This consular district includes the following provinces/regions of China: Guizhou, Sichuan Xizang (Tibet), and Yunnan, as well as the municipality of Chongqing.

> Number 4, Lingshiguan Road, Section 4,
> Renmin Nanlu, Chengdu 610041
> Telephone: (86-28) 558-3992, 555-3119, after-hours (86-0) 13708001422
> Fax (86-28) 8558-3520
> E-mail l address is ACSchengdu@state.gov.

The Consular Section of the U.S. Consulate General in Shanghai

This consular district includes the following provinces/regions of China: Shanghai, Anhui, Jiangsu, and Zhejiang.

> The Westgate Mall, 8th floor,
> 1038 Nanjing Xi Lu, Shanghai 200031
> Telephone: (86-21) 3217-4650, ext. 2102, 2013, or 2134;
>   after-hours: (86-21) 6433-3936;
> Fax: (86-21) 6217-2071
> E-mail address: shanghai_acs@yahoo.com.

The U.S. Consulate General in Shenyang

This consular district includes the following provinces/regions of China: Liaoning, Heilongjiang, and Jilin.

> No. 52, 14th Wei Road
> Heping District, Shenyang 110003
> Telephone: (86-24) 2322-1198, 2322-0368;
>   after-hours: (86-0) 13704019790
> Fax (86-24) 2322-2374
> E-mail address is ShenyangACS@state.gov.

Other Offices

Alcoholics Anonymous can be reached in Beijing at telephone (86-10) 139-1138-9075

Al-Anon chapter in Beijing that can be reached at (86-10) 6940-3935.

Bureau of Citizenship and Immigration Services in the Department of Homeland Security BCIS web site—http://www.uscis.gov

Chinese Embassy in the United States
Embassy of the People's Republic of China
2300 Connecticut Ave., NW
Washington, DC 20008
Tel: 202-328-2500

China also has Consulates in Los Angeles, CA; San Francisco, CA; Chicago, IL; New York, NY, and Houston, TX.

Police)—010-8401-5292

Office of Children's Issues—recorded information regarding changes in adoption procedures and general information, 1-888-407-4747.

Our Chinese Daughter's Foundation—Beijing Office—011-8610-6407-9687

State Department Visa Office—recorded information concerning immigrant visas for adoptive children, (202) 663-1225. A valid passport and visa are required to enter China.

Other Emergency Numbers:

Police	110
Fire	119
Ambulance	120 or 999

Adoption Travel

Visas must be obtained from Chinese Embassies or Consulates before traveling to China. Once you have been given travel approval, your adoption agency will give you a confirmed travel date. Do not make any travel arrangements that could result in a cancellation fee or that are nonrefundable. Airline tickets should be flexible because return dates could change.

Some airlines and hotels offer adoption rates, always ask. When making travel arrangements, consider travel agencies that have experience working with adoptive families. They will have experience making arrangements with short notice and will know who is offering the best deal at the time. Your agency should be able to give you recommendations and will frequently make part or all of the travel arrangements for you.

Once you arrive in the province you will have to meet with various government officials, sign documents, or possibly have a brief interview. A notary, who has much more authority in China, as it is an important government position, will complete the adoption. You may be granted custody of your child at that time or the following business day.

All rules regarding adoption procedures, including the amount of time you are required to remain in the country are subject to change at any time. Some countries have better records than others have regarding policy changes; these changes rarely occur without some warning. Rumors regarding adoption policy and changes in procedures are rampant. Consider the source and rely on your agency to address these rumors as necessary.

During your stay, try to do as much sightseeing as possible and absorb your child's culture. Visit museums, sample local cuisine; attend the ballet or opera; explore tourist areas or other famous landmarks or memorials. While in Beijing, visit Tiennaman Square, the Great Wall and the Forbidden City. You may also be able to visit the orphanage or the location where your daughter was found. This may be a once in a lifetime opportunity, take advantage of it.

Your travel options will vary slightly by adoption agencies but will be on average 10-14 days. A typical travel scenario is

Day 1—Leave the U.S.

Day 2—Arrive in China (Most people arrive in Beijing)

Day 3—Tour Beijing (This may be optional) Allow 2 days minimum

Day 5—Leave for Province

Day 9—Travel to Guangzhou

Day 12—Return Home

Some areas of China, notably Yunnan and Xinjiang Provinces, are prone to earthquakes, floods and rock falls along popular hiking trails. Coastal areas subject to typhoons during the summer rainy season include Hainan, Guangdong, Fujian, and Zhejiang Provinces are Travelers should check weather conditions for cities and areas in China prior to departure. Winter weather and typhoons can cause the closure of airports in some parts of the country.

Air Travel

Depending on the airline you choose, you may be able to fly coach/economy, business, or first class. Some international airlines may offer business class seating equivalent to what we consider first class, and they are often no more expensive than a coach seat on another airline. On return flights that are not full, flight attendants will sometimes upgrade adoptive families.

Consider traveling as direct a route as possible. This will help minimize your travel time and decrease the risk of missing connecting flights. Once you have been granted custody of your daughter, you will be anxious to return home. Don't add additional travel or sightseeing to the end of your trip. Doing so, will only add additional confusion and time to adjust for your daughter.

When flying on an airline that is not American owned or operated, investigate their smoking policy. This is especially important if you or someone in your party has asthma or smoke allergies. Smoke may be more prevalent in economy or coach seating on some international flights. You may be able to upgrade to business, or first class.

Make sure that the person booking your tickets understands that you will be traveling with a small child. You can request bulkhead seating, which offers more legroom and sometimes a foldout bassinet. You should request a child's meal in advance if you are adopting a toddler or older child. When traveling with a small child, it may be necessary to enlist the help of the airline between connecting flights.

Many airlines offer adoption rates. However, it is not uncommon for travel agents or airline personnel to be unaware of these discounts. If you know that an airline does offer adoption fares, it may be necessary to speak to a supervisor or someone who is more knowledgeable in discounting rates. If you have been quoted an outrageously priced ticket, look around before committing, most likely you will be able to find a better rate.

In addition to being given customs declaration of your flight, you will also be given arrival and health forms to complete. You may want to make a quick trip to the bathroom shortly before landing as you will have to make several stops before you can clear customs. First you must go to the Health Inspection desk and give them your completed health form. Secondly, you will go through Immigration. They will need your completed arrival card, your passport, and Visa. Once it has been determined that you may enter the country, you may then go to luggage pickup and proceed to customs. If you have nothing to declare you will go through the green lane and enter into China.

Prior to returning home, you will want to change your Chinese money back to U.S. Dollars. Remember you must save the exchange receipts to do this. When it is time to leave, You will exit through customs and immigration. You will have to fill out a departure card at the airport which will be turned in at this time. Your Visa will be invalidated.

Children over two years of age must have their own seats in an aircraft regardless of their size. While it is not required, it is recommended by the Federal Aviation Administration (FAA) that all children under forty pounds ride in a FAA-approved child safety restraint system. Children under forty pounds will not fit in an airline seat properly. It may be logistically impossible to carry a child seat with you, and most likely it will be impossible to keep a toddler buckled in any type seat for any extended period. If your daughter is not buckled in her seat and you experience turbulence, she should be buckled in immediately.

One alternative to taking a car seat is the Baby B'Air flight vest. It secures to your lap belt, may be used in flight, and is considered safer than holding a child in your arms. It is not allowed during takeoffs, landings, or taxiing in the United States. Check with your airline; some now provide child safety restraint systems. Families who travel with an FAA-approved child safety restraint may receive additional discounted tickets for their children.

Takeoffs and landings may be painful to little ears. One way to relieve air pressure is to give a child something to drink during this time. Avoid juice as it may cause upset stomach. Tea and un-carbonated beverages are best. If needed, you can shake the bubbles out of carbonated drinks.

For toddlers, try lollipops or safety pops. Older children may benefit from nausea pops that may help alleviate airsickness. Yawning will help release ear pressure and another alternative is earplugs or swimmer ear plugs. They are available in a child size for children under age six. Earplugs are small wax plugs that are placed over the ear opening as a cover. They do not go inside the ear itself. Getting ear plugs of any type in the ear or to be left in may be tricky but besides relieving ear pain they will also help to drown out noise.

Some adults may benefit from earplugs or "Ear Planes." Ear Planes help relieve ear pain, clogging or popping, and regulate air pressure. If you have frequent sinus pain or pressure, you may also benefit from taking sinus medication prior to air travel or thirty minutes to one hour before your final descent.

When you arrive in the US you will have to go through Immigration and Customs. The "mysterious" Visa package will be turned in to customs as this time, remember do not open this as it has been sealed. You should have completed a customs declaration form, listing purchases. Depending on how much and what you purchase you may be subject to paying Duty. Consult customs regulations prior to your trip.

Train Travel

Trains are rarely used by adoptive families in China. Most often they would only be used for families who have a return flight departing from Hong Kong. They may opt to take a train from Guangzhou to Hong Kong. In some cases, you will need to purchase an entire cabin and a facilitator or interpreter will travel with you.

Car Travel

On occasion, it may be necessary to travel by car or bus for several hours if your daughter is located in a more rural area. This can be an adventure in itself. Most likely there will be no rest areas or bathroom facilities. (Welcome to the great outdoors!) Roads may be in need of repairs or unpaved, people may drive on the opposite side of the road than you are used to, and weather conditions may be less than ideal.

People in many other countries do not use car seats for children. Most likely, you will not be able to use a car seat in a vehicle if you take one with you. Your daughter may have never ridden in a car and may experience motion sickness or be terrified.

Networking: Know the Area

Several factors will help determine the ease of adoption travel. Use an experienced adoption agency, and network with families who have traveled before you. There are a number of Internet resource groups for adoptive parents who have already completed or are in the process of completing an adoption.

You should be able to find families who have adopted from the same province that you are adopting from. Try to find families who have traveled most recently so you can obtain the most current information. You may want to know about the following subjects:

- Appropriate dress
- Availability of products: toiletries, baby items, bottled water, etc.
- Cash, credit cards, American dollar conversion
- Adoption procedures
- Customs
- Embassy visit
- Emergency contact or an independent or non-agency-affiliated interpreter
- General safety concerns
- Hotel and homestay options
- Internet access
- Medical care

- Length of stay
- Options for phoning home
- Orphanage observation and needs
- Places to shop, regional souvenirs
- Places to visit and things to do
- Restaurants, food safety
- Travel options, how they got there

Chapter 18

Packing for Your Trip

Suitcases, Handbags, and Luggage

Many people have legitimate concerns that their luggage will arrive and arrive undamaged. If you must purchase new luggage for your trip, consider luggage with sturdy wheels. Seasoned travelers will often recommend hard-sided luggage over soft-sided. Cloth luggage may easily be torn, and hard sides prevent thieves from cutting it open and stealing your things. However hard-sided luggage will weigh more.

I recommend the use of basic black or dark-colored luggage. Use discretion—no red, tapestry, or animal-print luggage. Although it may take longer to find at baggage claim, you want your luggage to blend not draw attention to itself. Luggage tags are required on both carry-on and checked luggage for travelers to China.

Luggage locks are all similar, and most can be opened easily. Whichever type you choose, consider replacing the locks. But a note of warning: if you fly in the US your locks may be cut off if your bags are searched. You may want to use plastic closures that may be cut off and replaced by security. When you arrive in China you will be required to use luggage locks. Take a few extra locks, in case any are lost or broken.

In China, each person is allowed one bag per person. Traveling light is imperative. In China luggage can not weigh more than 44 pounds per person on domestic flights and 65 pounds on International flights. In order to be safe, do not go over forty pounds. You will need to pre-weigh your luggage to make sure you did not go over capacity. Do not take a large suitcase which may be difficult to carry when filled to capacity, and will put you over weight capacity.

A medium suitcase no larger than 26 inches should be all you need. It should be light enough to carry as needed. You may have to carry your luggage for some distance without the use of wheels in unpaved parking lots, while climbing stairs, and so on.

In recent years, airline policy has changed regarding carry-on bags, and you should check for each airline's requirements. For travelers to China, most will only allow one carry-on bag per person. This may be a fifteen-inch carry-on bag, or a backpack. I recommend for a party of two to take one of each as the backpack can act as a diaper bag on the return trip home.

If there is room in your carry-on bags, you may want to try to include one change of clothing per family member, a couple of your gift items, and assorted toiletries. You should also split your belongings between your checked bags. At the very least, each person should have a set of clothes in each bag. You may also split gift items and donations between bags.

A handbag or pocketbook may count as one piece of carry-on luggage. If you purchased a seat for your child, then you may be allowed to bring an equal allocation of carry-on luggage for her on the return flight. While a stroller or a diaper bag would most likely be counted as one piece of carry-on luggage, a child safety seat would not.

No traveler wants to arrive at her destination only to find that her luggage has been lost or stolen. To avoid serious problems, hand-carry all adoption documents, including visas and passports. (Carry extra copies in your checked baggage as well.) All necessary prescription medication should be included in your carry-on luggage.

When possible, carry identification, cash, and credit cards on you. Travel wallets, worn around the neck or waist and inside clothing are much safer than a money belt, belt bag, or fanny pack. Any time you are in a crowded area be aware of potential pickpockets. This includes groups of young children.

Handbags or wallets are fair came for thieves. If you must carry a small handbag try a wallet on a string that can be worn across your chest, shoulder to hip, under your coat or jacket. No one can come up behind you and grab your bag, and it will rest on your hip where you can easily reach in or hold it.

Do not take bottled water or soft drinks. It is heavy to carry and can easily be bought once you are there. If you take it with you, it will most likely be opened at customs. To help eliminate bulkiness and weight of items, consider taking travel size, half-full or smaller containers. You can put some items in plastic zippered bags. Rather than taking boxes, you can cut the label out or fold the box to pack flat.

Don't pack nail files, scissors, razors, or pocketknives in carry-on luggage. If possible, wear a bra that does not have underwire. If you have a clothing item that has caused problems (I have a pair of boots that set off security alarms), do not wear it while traveling.

Sometimes adoptive families who will be traveling together decide to pool supplies. One will plan on bringing all the diapers, another brings wipes and yet another brings other critical supplies. This is probably a really bad idea, especially if your luggage gets lost or misses a flight. Imagine arriving with no diapers for your babies.

Because most essentials are readily available in china it is no longer necessary to stockpile baby items but should pack enough to get you through a few days and buy the rest as needed.

Health Care and Toiletries

In many parts of the world, personal need items such as soap or diapers are readily available, while other items such as baby wipes or disposable training pants will not be. Be prepared and plan ahead; you may have little or no choice in selecting a brand name.

You may need to pack some or all of the following:

- Adult wipes
- Alcohol Wipes (to clean eating utensils)
- Antibacterial hand soap (and or wipes)
- Bath soap
- Bug spray
- Cordless curling iron
- Cotton balls
- Cotton swabs
- Cough drops
- Deodorant
- Eyedrops
- Hair brush/comb
- Hair dryer
- Hydrocortisone
- Lip balm
- Lotion (dual purpose-hand and body)

- Mouthwash
- Nail clippers
- Personal hygiene items
- Petroleum jelly
- Razor
- Sanitary Protection
- Scissors
- Shampoo and Conditioner
- Shower shoes
- Sunscreen
- Thermometer
- Tissues (small packs to use for toilet paper)
- Toilet paper (1 roll)
- Toothbrush/toothpaste
- Towels and washcloths
- Tweezers
- Vitamins

For your child, pack the following:

- Baby Powder (to help avoid heat rash)
- Baby shampoo
- Baby suppositories
- Baby thermometer
- Baby wipes
- Bath toys
- Bulb aspirator
- Cold medicine
- Diaper bag
- Diaper rash medication
- Diapers/disposable training pants
- Disposable changing pads

- Gas medication
- Hooded towels
- Lotion (unscented for extra dry, sensitive skin)
- Nail clippers
- Pacifiers
- Pain reliever
- Plastic training pants
- Potty chair
- Sunscreen
- Teether or teething ring
- Teething medication
- Tooth brush (Finger toothbrush)
- Tooth paste
- Tongue depressor
- Vitamins (without iron-until home-will help prevent constipation)

Medications

You should take all prescription medication in the original bottles along with copies of your prescription or the patient advisory information sheets, which usually include the doctor's name, pharmacy information, and the use for the medication. I prefer taking the patient advisory because it provides information concerning the use of the medication as well as doctor and pharmacy information. Take an extra copy of written prescription for medication and eyeglasses.

Most likely, you will need to consult your physician for prescriptions for medication that you can take with you such as a broad-based antibiotic to treat infection, prescription-strength antibiotic ointment, hydrocortisone, medication for the treatment of scabies, and possibly a tongue depressor for use at your child's embassy medical exam. In addition you may wish to take prescription diarrhea medication.

When you consult with and select a pediatrician for your daughter, she will give you her recommendations for any medications and dosages. You should obtain a prescription for an un-reconstituted antibiotic for your daughter. You want medication that has not been pre-mixed with water. Once it is mixed, most will need refrigeration. Because size information may be incorrect, or your daughter may be small for her age; use weight, not age recommendations for medication dosages. A note of caution: Do not use this prescription medication for your daughter without first consulting a physician (phone consultation, the embassy, or a local physician).

It is sometimes suggested to give young children cough, cold, or allergy medication to help them rest or sleep while traveling. However, this could have the opposite effect and cause hyperactivity or increased activity in young children. Most medications for children contain dye, and your daughter has probably not been exposed to this previously. There is a small risk of an allergic reaction to any medication. This is not something you want to occur at 30,000 feet.

If you have an overactive respiratory system, asthmatic cough, or asthma (even if it is very mild), include an asthma inhaler on your packing list. Air quality and pollution may be more than what you are used to.

Take a basic first-aid kit with you. You will also need to take many nonprescription medications to supplement your first-aid kit. You may wish to purchase the Pediatric Medical Travel Kit. (Formerly called the Texas Medical Kit) Available from Orphan Allies, it was designed for adoptive parents to cover medical conditions that are frequently seen in children adopted from China and other countries. It can be found at http://www.orphanallies.org/pediatricmedicalkit.html.

Here are a few first aid essentials:

- Anti-diarrhea medication
- Aspirin and/or aspirin substitute (*Never* give young children aspirin.)
- Assorted adhesive bandages
- Allergy medication
- Cough and cold medicine
- Earwax softener (Most likely, your child will have significant buildup.)
- Laxatives
- Lice-killing shampoo
- Lotion for sensitive skin (including eczema or dermatitis)
- Medication dispenser (medicine dropper, spoons, or syringe)
- Nausea medication
- Oral rehydration liquid or powder

- Rubbing alcohol or hydrogen peroxide (both available in swab form)
- Saline nose drops
- Scabies medication
- Sinus medication
- Syringes
- Triple Antibiotic ointment
- Upset stomach, heartburn, or indigestion medication

Food to Take Along

Traveling abroad and trying new cuisine will be a whole new dining experience. This includes reading the menu, ordering, paying, and tipping, proper etiquette, and cultural protocol. Larger cities will have restaurants with English menus. Practice using chopsticks ahead of time.

You may be served what you consider breakfast foods for lunch or dinner and vice versa. Because it may not be something that you are used to eating, it may not always agree with you, and you may find that you like the food considerably or dislike it. Do not eat from street vendors.

Because American based restaurants such as McDonald's, Pizza Hut and Kentucky Fried Chicken can be found in larger cities. Most of your personal food needs should be minimal, (unless you are very picky) Do not bring more than a few essentials or favorite snacks along with you. Most familiar snack foods are readily available in China. Comfort foods that travel well include crackers, cheese in a can, coffee, instant soup, peanut butter, and oatmeal.

In addition to baby food and snacks, you may need an assortment of silverware, dinnerware, sippy cups, and bibs (consider disposable ones) for your child. You may consider bringing plastic, disposable silverware and anti-bacterial dish soap.

Food for Your Baby

Plan on continuing your daughter's current diet as much as possible until you return home. Travel, a new environment, and food sensitivity can all play a role in your daughter's reaction to new foods. When I was told my daughter had never had juice before, I should have heeded that warning. Instead we gave her a host of new foods, and not all of them agreed with her. If your daughter is older and able to eat many table foods, play it safe, start slow and bland.

Soy formula is frequently recommended, and powdered varieties are easier to carry with you. If you will be using formula, you will need bottles, assorted nipples, and possibly a measuring cup. Babies may not like disposable bottles because the nipples are not what they are used to. They are used to large nipples, or ones with a "fast flow" Some adoptive families recommend "nuk" style while others have used standard nipples.

You may decide not to switch nipples while you are in China but to purchase while you are there. You can buy enough to get you home and then transition once you get home.

Baby food is usually packaged in glass jars and can be quite heavy. You probably do not want to take any with you. You can cut up most foods as long as you take into account the size of the food and number of teeth your daughter has. Your guide can help you find familiar foods for your daughter such as rice congee or steamed eggs and help you purchase anything else you may need once you assess your daughter's dietary needs.

Rice cereal is a good starter food and will most likely be similar in substance to some foods your child is accustomed to eating. You may have to play with the amount of water or milk that is added. If your daughter refuses to eat, try making it a different thickness. Callie loved baby cereal but would eat it only if it was very thick.

Popular kid snacks include cheddar crackers, individual-serving cereal boxes, animal crackers, and other beginner food products. Avoid caffeine, chocolate, and foods or juice that are heavy in sugar, preservatives, or dyes. All of these can cause hyperactivity in children, and there is a good chance that your daughter has never been exposed to any of them.

No meal would be complete without numerous feeding essentials:

- Bottles with disposable insert—(2-4) eight ounce bottles (2) four ounce
- Disposable bottles (40)
- Feeding Spoon
- Insulated bottle holder
- Kitchen tongs for bottle
- Mug
- Nipples (about 8 in assorted styles)
- Plastic bowl
- Plastic container for formula

- Quart size plastic bottle
- Silverware
- Thermos (wide mouth)

Food for You

If you have special dietary restrictions, you may consider taking an assortment of foods. Sugar substitute and coffee creamer may not be available. If you are a coffee or tea drinker, you may want to take your drink of choice along with you as well as a hot pot.

If you have a favorite food, it should be on your must-take list. If you have comfort foods that you eat when you are tired, sick, or feeling blue, you most likely will want to pack these as well. (Sorry, ice cream can't go in a suitcase.) Consider taking peanut butter, instant or canned soup, or small containers of canned fruit. You cannot take fresh fruit into another country, and it may or may not be readily available.

My favorites included applesauce, which saved me the day that we had a stomach virus. Ketchup, a necessity that I did not take enough of, was available but did not taste the same. I found that pretzels and cheese crackers pack better than some chips or crackers (it may depend upon the container), and I wish that I had taken more chocolate-covered peanuts. Cereal/fruit bars do not travel well.

Clothing to Pack

You will want to pack weather-appropriate clothing that respects the customs and traditions of your host country. Taste and discretion in your clothing choices are good rules to follow. Think business casual. Suits or dresses are not necessary. You should include at least one pair of khaki or dark chino pants or skirt, and polo shirts.

You may find that you want or need to visit several different cites or provinces. These will probably include Beijing, the province where your child is residing and to Guangzhou when you visit the U.S. Embassy to receive your visa before returning home. Temperatures and weather may vary.

There are many myths as there are opinions about proper dress for adoption travel. Some travelers to China say "no skirts" others say "wear skirts". Being fashion-conscious, I was worried about all the things that I had heard and spent way to much time and energy worrying about inappropriate clothing when we adopted Callie.

The type of clothing considered appropriate may vary from one city or region to the next. Some will be tourist destinations or resort cities that are accustomed to tourists. More traditional or rural locations require more conservative clothing.

You will be judged by how you conduct yourself and how you are dressed. Clothing should show proper respect. It is usually not considered appropriate to wear jeans or shorts when visiting government offices. In addition, do not wear shorts to meetings, ceremonies, to interviews or if you get to visit the orphanage.

More versatility in dressing may be obtained by choosing a skirt set and other clothing that can coordinate with it. This will give you flexibility and clothing options while packing a minimal number of pieces. Take items that can be layered and are wrinkle resistant. Most likely, you will need to take two-three complete outfits per person, not including the outfit you are wearing. We also took several articles of clothing that would coordinate with other items to give us 4—5 days of coordinating clothing. With these, we could dress up or down as needed. I chose a dressy sheer cardigan that would give my black skirt and blouse an evening look. Leave most jewelry at home.

Comfortable basic walking shoes are essential. Take two pairs to alternate. Sandals should be okay depending on the time of year you travel but you may end up with dirty, dusty or wet feet. Tennis shoes or other sport shoes may or may not be considered appropriate. It may depend on their color. White shoes would be much more noticeable than black ones. You may want to take slippers to wear when you are in your hotel and possibly shower shoes or flip-flops for the shower.

Sweat suits, shorts, and T-shirts are only suitable for lounging in your hotel room. Jeans should be okay to wear while traveling or during other non-business aspects of your trip, but don't take more than one pair. Black denim will provide you with a more sophisticated look than blue.

Warm-Weather Travel

The weather in China can be vastly different from one region to another. In summer months it is very hot and humid and includes dry seasons and monsoons.

Areas that are accustomed to warm weather would be more prepared for providing relief from the heat. In addition to taking essentials, you may want to pack several extra tops and underwear. If it's very hot, you may need to change clothes more often.

Lightweight, breathable fabrics are best. Natural fabrics may be cooler than synthetic ones, but they will not travel as well and may wrinkle easily. Cotton is more travel friendly than linen or linen blends. Skirts may be cooler than pants and look nicer, too. Shoes should be comfortable; remember that excessive heat may cause your feet to swell. Use caution when considering sandals or other open-toed shoes.

During warm weather you may want to opt for minimal makeup, light or no perfume, and easy to care for hairstyles, or wash and go perm. (Sorry, no hot curlers allowed) we often remember to bring hats for baby but in hot weather many people choose to wear hats; perfect for a bad hair day.

You may have the opportunity to visit beaches and lakes or use hotel pools if you are traveling during summer months. My husband decided to take a swimsuit since we were traveling in midsummer, and one of our hotels had an indoor pool. At the last minute I threw mine in the suitcase since there was enough room. I was very happy to have made this decision after a week of 100-degree weather and no air-conditioning.

A sweater or jacket should be taken for use on the plane, indoor locations that are blessed with air conditioners, or where it is common to find a large discrepancy in day and evening temperatures.

A basic warm-weather wardrobe for women should include the following:

- 1 skirt
- 1 pair shorts or capri pants
- 2 pair of casual pants (could include 1 jean or capri pants)
- 1 blouse
- 1 two-piece cardigan set
- 2 knit shirts
- 1 light/crocheted sweater or jacket
- 1-2 pairs of shoes
- 5 pairs of underwear
- 1-2 pairs of pajama's

Extra items could include a pair of shorts and a knit shirt, a swimsuit, and a dressy blouse or sweater.

For men, the wardrobe should include these items:

- 1 or 2 pairs of shorts
- 1-2 pairs of casual pants
- 1 pair of jeans
- 2 casual knit shirts
- 2 polo or collared shirts
- 1 light weight jacket
- 5 pairs of underwear
- 1-2 pairs of pajamas
- 1-2 pairs of shoes

Cold-Weather Travel

You should be able to find current weather forecasts from a variety of sources to help you make your selections when packing. Unless you are traveling to climates with mild winters, winter coats should be full-length.

Hats are a basic requirement during winter months. Plan on taking a good pair of gloves and a scarf. Boots should be lined and water-resistant, and you should plan on taking a second pair of shoes wherever you go to change into when you go inside.

Lightweight thermal underwear may be necessary, and tights and leggings can be worn under pants or skirts for extra warmth. You may need to insulate yourself for warmth outside, but it may be very warm inside. It may be necessary to remove a layer or two of clothing whenever you are indoors. You do not want to wear just a thermal shirt underneath a wool sweater, because you would probably not be able to remove your sweater as needed.

A basic cold-weather wardrobe for women should include:

- 2 pairs of casual pants or skirts
- 1 pair of denim pants
- 2 long sleeve tops
- 1 turtleneck sweater
- 1 turtleneck
- 1 wool blazer or cardigan sweater
- 1 sweater

The wardrobe for men should include:

- 2 pairs of casual pants
- 1 pair of jeans
- 2 long-sleeved knit shirt
- 1 oxford shirt
- 1 turtleneck
- 1 sweater or cardigan or sweater vest
- 1 pullover sweater

Clothing for Your Child

You will need to provide all of your child's clothing needs. The clothing you will need for your child will be similar to what you need. These items include pajamas, underwear and undershirts, thermals, coats or snowsuits, scarves, hats, gloves or mittens, street clothes, sweaters or jackets, shoes, and socks. (See Chapter 5, "The Wardrobe.")

When your adoption is completed, it is a special occasion and most likely you will want to pack a special "going home/leaving the hospital" outfit for your daughter. One to take first pictures of you and your child or for your daughter to wear when you arrive home.

Your child's caretakers will be watching closely to make sure that your child is appropriately dressed. Less is not more, and you will need to provide the appropriate number of layers deemed necessary for your child to be adequately protected from the elements.

Toddlers and infants are not allowed outdoors in many societies without a hat, and failing to bring one or have your child wear one may mean that you proceed at your own risk. More than a few unknowing Americans have been scolded for these offenses.

Laundry

Because you will be limited in the amount of clothing that you will be able to pack, you will want to take wrinkle-resistant clothing in quick-drying wash-and-wear fabrics. Plan on doing at least part or all of your laundry yourself, for this you will need a small box of laundry detergent, a clothesline, and a sink stopper.

Powdered detergent is best. Most likely, you will not be able to use tablets since most of your wash will be done in your sink. For delicates, take liquid delicate care cleaner or use shampoo. For example, shampoo for color-treated hair is designed specifically to stay colorfast. Most laundries sell small travel-size or single-use packages of detergent. Pack detergent in a zippered bag to prevent spills. You may want to take baby detergent to wash your daughter's clothes in.

Cotton and polyester fabrics dry fastest. A hairdryer can be used to dry some clothes. Stain removing wipes can be used for spot cleaning clothing in between washes.

Laundry service is usually fast but may be expensive. Laundry is usually done in very hot water which can cause shrinkage or fading in some fabrics. When we adopted Callie, same-day laundry service was available at several of our three hotels. We would give the hotel staff our clothes in the morning and they were returned to us clean in the evening. You should budget between $50.00 to $100.00 for laundry expenses. Don't forget to ask for discounts on children's clothes.

Miscellaneous

In addition to clothing, toiletries, and food, there are many other items that you may want to consider taking with you on your travels. Space and weight will determine how and what you ultimately decide to take. Buy what you need upon arrival when possible. If you buy a seat on the plane for your daughter on the return home flight, you may take an additional piece of luggage.

Paper Products and Stationery

You may want to record the adoption process in a journal so you have a history of events. If you choose to do this, take your journal with you when you travel so that you can write about your adoption experiences while they are fresh in your mind. There is a good possibility that after you get home, you will not have time to do this.

Another great idea is to take a notebook with consulate information, emergency contact numbers, and any questions that you may have or to write down information that you receive about your child. Attach removable temporary adhesive notes to documents that you may need to help you find them and remember what they are.

We took blank stationery and asked that orphanage workers write notes, information, and/or stories about our child. We were thrilled to receive six personal letters about our daughter.

Cash or Charge

All cash should be crisp, clean, new bills. If not, try to get bills in the best condition possible. Cash that is old and worn may not be accepted. Your facilitator will advise you when, how, and in what currency to pay. For general use do not exchange more than $100.00 at a time, unless otherwise instructed. When you make exchange money at a Foreign Exchange Counter, Get receipts and save them. At the airport, at end of your trip, you may be able to exchange any foreign currency that you have not spent.

Take an assortment of denominations, but the bulk of them will probably need to be $100 bills. You will need some smaller bills for miscellaneous expenses such as tipping and for use while traveling in the States. Also, when traveling abroad, it is not uncommon for vendors who wish to be paid in U.S. dollars not to have change in U.S. dollars.

You will need to research whether you can use credit cards or traveler's checks. This will vary by city, region, and country. Most larger hotels take credit cards but you will need to use cash everywhere else. Visa or American Express traveler's checks can be cashed in banks or some hotels for a small fee. Traveler's checks are a smart choice as a way to take most of your money. The exception would be of fees paid to the Chinese government and orphanage donations. You would need cash for this. There is usually a $200.00 limit on cashing travelers checks.

Do not plan on using credit cards for most purchases. Exchange rates for credit cards can be high but you will need to use it for room incidental deposits at hotels. Hotels, larger stores and Friendship Stores will take credit cards. Visa and American Express are most readily accepted. Notify your credit card company that you will be traveling abroad. If your credit card company sees charges that are made overseas, they may call your home to verify the transactions. Because you will not be at home to do this, your charge privileges may be suspended. Make sure that you have your PIN number with you as well in case you need it.

You should also inquire about conversion fees for purchases made in a foreign currency. The Bank of China determines the exchange rate. The unit of currency in China is the RMB. You may wish to pick up a conversion sheet before doing any shopping.

Make a list of Traveler's Check numbers and Credit Card numbers, including whom to call if they are lost or stolen. Leave one copy at home with whomever you have designated as your emergency contact and take the other copy with you. Carry all money, Credit cards, traveler's checks, etc. on your person. Do not give to beggars and be very cautious with groups of small children.

Tipping

In China, tipping is the norm and you should tip those in the service industry such as a luggage carriers, divers and guides. Tips generally are $1.00 to $3.00 dollars per person per day and will depend on the person's job title and the length of time you use their services. Consult with your guide.

Calling Long Distance

Your travel destination will predetermine your ability to use calling cards, phone cards, a cell phone, or computer equipment. In many cases, your local long distance carrier will be able to provide this service. When researching your phone options, make sure you document your conversation, including your contact spoke and the rate they quoted. This will help in case there are any problems when you receive your phone bill.

You can charge calls to your room or your home phone but service fees vary and can be expensive. Pre-paid phone cards are also a good option to use while you are in China. Cell phones, which can be used for international phone calls, are becoming more popular and may be a viable option. You may wish to rent a Panda Phone: a mobile phone that you can pick up in both the US and in China. It comes with a calling card option for domestic and international use. See www.pandaphone.com

Always carry important phone numbers with you: Chinese contacts, the American Consulate/Embassy, attorneys, doctors, friends and family, insurance company, adoption agency contacts in the U.S and in China, social worker, the airline, your travel agent, a fax number at home, and possibly even your local congressman or senators office.

Documents and Other Valuables

Most valuables, including wedding and engagement rings and other fine jewelry, should be left at home. Play it safe and simple with jewelry; take one or two pairs of inexpensive, basic earrings.

Take copies of adoption documents as well as passports and visas. Keep them separate from the originals. This may include giving your facilitator copies or putting copies in a hotel safe.

You may wish to carry important documents such as Power of Attorney (one for each spouse) and take plastic sleeves to put important documents in, as well as a copy of your itinerary.

Batteries, Cameras, and Converters

Make sure to pack your camera and video recorder, as well as an ample supply of film flashcards, and batteries. Avoid buying or developing film in China. Commercial filming equipment may require a permit for use. Flash photography indoors is usually not allowed, especially when sightseeing. You may want to take more than one camera in case something happens to one. Carry film and insist that it not be x-rayed as the machines or lead cases may be unreliable.

Hong Kong and Mainland China both use 220V, 50 HZ electrical power. You will need a converter for a battery charger. Some appliances have flip switches but most likely, you will need a converter, or plug adapter for hair dryers or various other appliances. Avoid hair dryers and curlers, etc. If you must have you can purchase them while you are their and they are very inexpensive.

Use caution when using converters. Beware of sockets that look worn. Never try to repair them. For conversation information and equipment, see www.magellans.com

Laptop and Internet Use

Unless you take your laptop everywhere you go or must conduct business while you are traveling; you may want to leave it at home. It will be heavy to carry, and you will have to leave it in your hotel room the majority of the time.

You may find an Internet café to communicate with friends, family, or physicians while abroad. Many Internet cafés charge a minimal fee and can be much less expensive than calling long distance. Most digital cameras will not work at an Internet café. You may not be able to send pictures or videos, depending on your location.

Most hotels have a business center or rooms have DSL high speed access with Internet access. You may need to take a travel adapter plug—extra phone connection.

Do not forget to bring e-mail addresses with you. When someone sends you an e-mail at your hotel, it will be sent to you in the form of a printed message.

Make sure senders include your family name and the room number you are in the text of the message.

Leisure Time

Chances are you will not be able to find a television that broadcasts in English. With the exception of larger cities which may have CNN or BBC. Leisure time may vary. You may have very little spare time, or you may spend a lot of time in your hotel room.

Bring at least one good book. It may be hard to find any in English. Other actives may include playing cards, hobbies such as cross-stitch, or business-related activities.

Other Items

Other miscellaneous items you may want to bring include the following:

- Baby care or children's medical book
- Bubble wrap
- Calculator or currency conversion chart
- Duct tape
- Duffel bag (cheap fold-up one to make room for extra's purchased)
- Foreign language phrase book
- Infant or child carrier
- Insect repellent
- Map
- Mailing labels (pre-printed, peel and stick to send postcards)
- Mailing tube
- Nightlight
- Notebook paper
- Photo album to show
- Pillow cases
- Plastic trash bags
- Pocket Notebook
- Rubber bands

- Sewing kit
- Shopping bags
- Small flashlight
- Stroller/umbrella stroller
- Tape
- Travel alarm clock
- Travel guide
- Umbrella
- White-out pen
- Zippered plastic bags—all sizes

Miscellaneous items for baby

- Baby bath tub (Inflatable)
- Baby blankets (2)
- Baby sling—or other carrier
- Diaper bag
- Hooded towels (2)
- Stroller
- Washcloths (2)

Chapter 19

While You are There

It is not unusual for families to find that adoption travel is the first time they travel outside the country. You may notice differences from the time you board your plane. Airline instructions may be given in English as well as another language. It would not be unusual to find that many people on your plane are native to your host country and that you may be an English-speaking minority.

When you land, you may be disoriented as a result of jet lag, anticipation, unfamiliar surroundings, or insecurity at not knowing the language. It can be intimidating to enter a foreign country, especially if you are greeted by armed guards at the gates before going through passport control and customs.

In most cases an agency representative will meet you as soon as you go through customs. Keep your emergency contact numbers handy in case you are not able to find your contact. Most agencies wish to provide clients with the best possible service, and your safety is of the utmost concern.

Most likely, you will have a driver, interpreter, and or a guide who will be take you to your appointments and some sightseeing. Sometimes a driver will act as the interpreter as well. If two families or more are completing an adoption simultaneously, they may be able to split the fees.

It may be possible to shop or sightsee without their services, and they will give you recommendations. On occasion, this may be based on political climate and world events. If you are using a taxi without assistance, then you can need to get address you are going to written down to give to the driver. Don't forget to get the return address, or that of your hotel.

Do not be afraid to go out. Use common sense and defer to your guides expertise. They will tell you about the surrounding area and things that you can do on your own. Try to absorb everything around you; this is a trip of a lifetime. You will see many things for the first and possibly only time. The sights, sounds, and even smells may take some getting used to. No amount of preparation can ever truly prepare you for this trip.

It would not be uncommon to experience some type of culture shock after you arrive. Differences in language, business conduct, values, and etiquette are the most common causes. While you may have your own stereotypes that you apply, they will like wise be applied to you. Americans are commonly thought of as being, wealthy, outspoken and demanding.

It is important to remmber that you are an ambassador for all adoptive parents and remmber to be flexible, and non-judgmental. It is important that you remain calm, avoid alcohol, public displays of affection, and most importantly never raise your voice in criticism of anyone Chinese. Being tardy is considered bad manners, as is showing impatience, finger pointing, and negative questions. Avoid discussing such topics as human rights, politics, sex, religion, and other political issues, especially social concerns and territorial disputes.

If you find yourself in any of the above situations, you may find it odd that people are smiling or laugh. Smiling does not necessarily mean that everything is okay, This may be due to the fact the person does not understand you or that that it is merely a polite way to cover up an embarrassing situation.

Many of China's customs and practices have derived from Confucian philosophy. Confucianism has influenced moral and ethical values. This includes respecting and deferring to elders, family history, tradition and responsibility. It is important that you acknowledge and respect the hierarchical relationships that have been established. Chinese are very conscious of their social status and you should make a point to always remember someones name and when you speak to them you should use their title and name.

Because social position is important, you will be seated accordingly when sharing a meal. If you are invited to a banquet, you will most likely be seated at a large round table. Persons on the right serve persons on their left. If your plate is empty someone may fill it for you. The first person to lead a toast is the top ranking person at the dinner. Other toast may follow; only after a toast has been made by the most senior member, at the head table who will toast the host. Drink alcohol sparingly. To become intoxicated is considered a disgrace to yourself and to your host.

During your meal, do not eat any food that has fallen on the tablecloth, do not put your fingers in your mouth, (not just mealtime but anytime) do not point your chopsticks, do not sit them on the table or place them across a bowl or plate. Always place your chopsticks on the chopstick holders, or pillows.

Adoption as Viewed by the People

The majority of people in China are very glad that the children are being adopted. You may find yourself in the unique position of being admired for what you are undertaking, even if it may be for the simple reason of wanting to parent a child.

Because the people of China care greatly about their children, you will find that most Chinese people are warm and friendly. They may approach you and say "lucky baby", or give you the thumb's up sign. They may offer you words of encouragement or give you childcare instructions.

As adoptive parents, it is our responsibility to be gracious and to conduct ourselves in an exemplary manner particularly while completing an adoption. You are, in a sense, an ambassador of good will for your country, and you set the standard on how adoptive parents are viewed.

Hotels

Hotel reservations are usually made by your adoption agency, and they frequently negotiate adoption rates for families. It is not uncommon to arrive and find other adoptive families staying at the same hotel and adoptive families using the same agency often travel together.

Hotels frequently include breakfast and may or may not have one or more restaurants. The hotel staff may or may not speak English. Hotels may offer a variety of services including restaurants, Karoke bars, nightclubs, swimming pools, exercise rooms, laundry services, and more.

Hotels considered moderate, budget, or economy might not be what we are used to by American standards. If you request a suite, it will usually consist of one bedroom, a small living area, and a bathroom. You may or may not have a kitchen but will probably have a refrigerator and a television.

You need to request a crib when you make the reservation; most will have cribs. If not, your child may have to sleep with you or you may have to be creative in finding another alternative.

If it is summer, you may have to request an air-conditioned room, if they are available. Windows may or may not have screens. You should do a basic safety inspection of your room to make sure that it will be safe for your child. Check electrical outlets, loose electrical cords, or cords on window blinds. Check windows and doors. Open windows, windows without screens, floor-level windows, and balcony doors all pose a danger to inquisitive toddlers.

Most large cities such as Beijing and Guangzhou have their share of four and five-star hotels. The White Swan is a perennial favorite of adoptive families it not only has playrooms for children in the hotel but also a pool. An added benefit is the "Going Home" Barbie that adoptive parents are greeted with when they check in. It features a Caucasian Barbie with an Asian baby.

Hotels may have security guards at the elevators, and you may have to show your hotel pass to be admitted onto the elevators. The biggest problem with safety and security is property theft. Do not leave valuables in your hotel room and keep your suitcases locked whenever you are out.

To help expedite your departure, you should clear your hotel tab the night before you leave.

Declining/Losing a Referral

Losing a referral is a possibility that many adoption professionals do not like to discuss. Unfortunately, having lost a referral from Russia and having experienced a domestic adoption fraud, it is a topic that I am too familiar with. Fortunately for you it rarely happens in a Chinese adoption.

Reasons for failure to complete an adoption can vary. Countries can issue moratoriums, change requirements, increase fees, or open and close their borders to adoption at will. The USCIS can refuse to issue a visa if they are not satisfied that the paperwork is legitimate.

It is possible that you may be faced with a difficult decision regarding the continuation of your adoption. Families have on very rare occasions been notified that the child they were planning to adopt has more severe medical issues.

Declining a referral is never easy and will require a great deal of soul searching. As painful as this may be, you must make a decision that is best for you, your family, and the child in question. In most cases, families who have declined a child have been able to continue with the adoption process and have been matched with a different child.

Losing a child during the adoption process is similar to having a death in the family. Adoptive parents, like birth parents, do not wait until the child is born or an adoption is complete to form attachments. Adoptive parent attachment is frequently misunderstood and under appreciated by those who have not personally experienced it. Adoption support groups may not be able to provide support either unless another member has experienced adoption loss.

The loss of a referral can cause a delay in pre-attachment to your child. Mary Lib Mooney, Executive Director of International Adoption Guides, lost the referral of a child during the Russian adoption process. She recommends "grief counseling for families who have experienced an adoption loss." On occasion, adoptive parents or prospective adoptive parents experience depression as a result of losing a referral.

As devastating as loss of a referral can be, most families who experience it will tell you that they went on to successfully adopt the child or children that were supposed to be theirs after all. If you experience an adoption loss, get up, dust yourself off, take the time you need to grieve, explore your options, seek help if necessary, and decide what is best for your family. It may have taken a lot of strength and determination, but eventually the paths they took led them to their children.

Fraud

Adoption fraud is a "cruel and unusual" crime. Good record keeping and documenting conversations during the process will help in the event an adoption falls through. Know what your contracts mean and get everything in writing, especially pertaining to the services provided and the policy regarding a failed adoption. Are monies prorated or do you get full credit toward another adoption? What are you entitled to if you decide to change agencies?

No one has the right to purposely defraud or misrepresent themselves or their agency during the adoption process. This includes negligence, lack of product knowledge (not understanding adoption procedure, laws or risk), inexperience, or purposeful criminal intent.

If you or someone you know has been victimized by an agency or individual, report it to the proper authorities. These agencies include the Better Business Bureau, the State Licensing Specialist, the state bar association (for attorneys), your local congressional offices, the consulate or embassy, or various adoption-related entities.

Questions for the Caretaker

This may be the only time you are able to get information from anyone who has personal knowledge of and has interacted with your child or who has access to your child's records. Make the most of it and ask as many questions as possible. Take notes or record it if possible. Make sure that your questions are answered to your satisfaction. This may be quite challenging when using an interpreter who may be speaking English as a second language, but it may be your only opportunity. Here are some questions to consider.

Medical and Family History

- What vaccinations has your daughter received?
- What medical testing has she had?
- What are her known medical problems, and the current diagnosis, prognosis or recommended treatment?
- What childhood illness or other illnesses has she had? Has she been hospitalized or had surgery?
- What is her average temperature?
- Are there any scars (what caused these?) or birthmarks?
- Are there any known allergies?
- How does the child act when sick?
- What was the medical diagnosis at birth?
- Was the child born premature or at full term?
- Is there any history of prenatal alcohol or drug exposure or abuse?
- How long has she been at the orphanage?
- Are there any special skills or therapy that we should observe/learn before we are granted custody?

Personal

- Is any personal information available about the birth family/siblings?
- What is her ethnic background?
- Where was she found?
- What was the date she was found?
- Who found her?
- At what age was she when she was found?
- Was there a note attached or any mementos?
- Who picked her name?
- What is the meaning and why was it chosen?
- Does she have a nickname?
- Does she have any personal possessions or things that are hers that we can keep and replace for you?

Daily Activities

- What is your daughter's daily routine?
- What time does she get up?
- When is bedtime and how long does she sleep?
- Does she nap? How often and how long?
- What type of bed does she sleep in?
- May we see her room/living quarters?
- Does she sleep in a room or bed with other children?
- Does she sleep on her tummy or back?
- Are the lights on or off and is it quiet or noisy?
- How much and how often does she eat?
- What foods does she like or dislike?
- What foods are served at typical meals?
- What about snacks or treats?
- Does she drink from a bottle or cup?
- Does she drink cow's milk or formula?
- Is she fed or does she feed herself?
- How does she react when she is tired or hungry?
- Is the child potty trained and what is her bathroom routine? How are baths given? (Tub or showers, hot or cold water?)
- When is playtime and what are her favorite playtime activities or toys?
- Does she spend time outside?
- Does she know numbers, letters, or colors?
- Has she ever been around animals: cats and dogs?
- Has the child ever ridden in a car, used a car seat?

Child Development

- Can your daughter talk or use other nonverbal communication?
- At what age did she reach developmental milestones: talking, walking, etc.?
- Is she afraid of anything, or do you have other emotional concerns?

- How is she comforted when upset?
- Is she attached to a caregiver? Does she have or has she had a favorite playmate?
- What are the names of caretakers/friends?
- Does she get along with other children, adults?
- Is she affectionate or dislike physical contact?
- Does she have good eye contact?
- How does she react when being scolded?
- What type of discipline is used? How does she respond?
- What is the child's normal personality? Shy, aggressive, outgoing?
- How does she compare to other children her age in the home?
- Does she have any likes or dislikes?
- How does she react when she is angry or frustrated?
- What is her personality like? Happy/melancholy?

Miscellaneous
- Has the child been baptized or participated in other religious ceremonies?
- Are there any keepsakes or records of this?
- Are there any photographs available?
- Are complete copies of her file available?
- Would anyone care to write a letter for your daughter?
- Is it possible to remain in contact with the orphanage or other associates/what is the address?
- What types of updates would they like to receive?

Orphanage Donations

Your adoption fees include orphanage donations and it is not necessary to make additional donations. Rather than making additional orphanage donations some families will choose to sponsor a child. This may be done thorough several programs such as Half the Sky Foundation or Love Without Borders. Because my daughter had a cleft lip/palate, I am particularly fond of programs that sponsor surgery for waiting children.

However if you choose to make a donation, they are always appreciated. The orphanage's need for basic essentials is far greater than luxury items. It was hard for us to plan for orphanage donations in advance because it was difficult to fully comprehend these needs without actually seeing them for yourself. We brought some gifts with us for the orphanage but bought many of the things that they needed once we arrived.

Some people choose to take money and buy what they need. This may include a large item that the orphanage needs such as a computer, stove or air conditioner. In addition arrangements can be made for caregiver training or to pay for a physician to visit the orphanage on a regular basis.

If you purchase donations in advance, shop at discount stores or stores that specialize in overruns. Look for end-of-season sales of overstocked merchandise. I once purchased infant and toddler boys' two-piece sweat suits for $3 from a local discount store and purchased approximately thirty summer outfits for around $75 in the fall. If you have children's clothing or merchandise manufacturers in your area, call them. Sometimes stores or business will donate new merchandise, seconds, or overruns to you or an organization that you may be affiliated with that is collecting orphanage donations.

You may get better results if you enlist the help of your office staff, women's club, school, or church to help collect donations. Don't think you can't ask for contributions. Instead you must decide that it never hurts to ask. I was able to get an extra 50 percent off summer clearance merchandise, toothbrushes from the dentist, and latex gloves from my doctor's office. My women's club at church collected orphanage donations as our international project, and my husband and I hand carried them to Russia.

I do not recommend taking plush animals. They are hard to clean, and I have seldom seen them in an orphanage. Toys should include animals and real people versus cartoon characters, monsters, or other creatures.

In most cases orphanage donations should be new items. Do not take previously used clothing or other items without permission from your adoption agency. If this is acceptable, they should be gently used and in good to excellent condition. Limit large bulky items such as diapers, which may be hard to pack, or other items that may be too heavy. You should be able to purchase diapers when you arrive.

Check to make sure any medication you plan to take for a donation is legal in your host country. If they are not legal, they may be confiscated by customs. Your agency should be able to tell you if a product can be used, if they have translated instructions for use, and whether the doctors would be familiar with its usage.

If you are taking a large amount of donations, it may be necessary to obtain a letter from your adoption agency stating that you are carrying orphanage donations. Having this letter with separately boxed items clearly marked *orphanage donations* or *humanitarian aid* may help you avoid paying customs fees. If you exceed luggage limitations, you may be charged for an extra container, by weight.

Ideas for donations include:

- Baby toiletries
- Cloth diapers
- Clothing
- Developmental toys
- Disposable diapers
- First-aid kits
- Medical equipment (thermometers(C Celsius)
- Medical supplies: medicine dropper, skin medication, fever medication, etc.
- Music cassettes (not CD's)
- School Supplies: crayons, markers, pencils, chalk, paper, coloring books.
- Undershirts
- Vitamins

Gifts

Gift giving as a way of expressing thanks or gratitude is quite common in many cultures but not expected or required in China. You may wish to purchase items for the children rather than for orphanage workers. Your agency will tell you for whom you may need to purchase gifts. You may need gifts for your facilitators, drivers, translators, orphanage workers, foster family, etc. You may also consider small gifts for hotel staff or tour guides.

Gifts do not have to be expensive but should be thoughtful and in good taste. Your facilitator will instruct you on how gift giving should be conducted. Gifts should include items that you would like to receive and should be useful. Gifts or items that we take for granted may be considered a luxury item. You should wait until after the adoption is completed to give gifts to people who may directly affect the adoption process.

Gifts should not be wrapped because they may be unwrapped at customs or baggage check. Gift bags and tissue pack easily, and the bags can be reused. Red and gold paper is considered appropriate for gift giving in China and small, clear cellophane party bags with designs on them can be purchased at most paper or party supply stores. Party bags can be filled ahead of time because they are see-through, and you should not have to open them. If you do need to open them, it is as simple as untying the ribbon. I used cloth ribbon to tie these with so that the recipient could reuse it.

Items that are homemade or native to where you live make great gifts, and it would be less likely that they may have been received before. Local goods, cassette tapes containing regional music or that of a local group or individual that you know, Native American jewelry or other items that may reflect your heritage, and books or souvenirs from your city or state all make unique gifts. It may also be possible to purchase items in China, such as flowers or chocolate that may be considered a luxury item.

Most gifts should cost between $5 to $25 and could include the following:

- American Ginseng
- Bottled dry spices
- Candy
- Car accessories
- Cigarettes
- Coffee and specialty teas
- Cookies
- Cosmetics/Perfume or cologne
- Gloves
- Flower seeds
- Hot chocolate
- Manicure sets
- Pens or pencil sets
- Scarves
- Scented Soaps
- Slippers

- Stationery/note cards
- Travel mugs

Souvenirs

Each city or province in China may have certain souvenir items that are unique. You may find that regional souvenirs may be a better quality and that the prices may be more reasonable than those found in larger cities and tourist areas.

In China there are both Government Department Stores and Private Department Stores. More and more private shops and shopping malls are opening and you can get many western items at these stores. Government Department stores are stores designed for the average person to be able to get the common household goods that they need.

Friendship Stores are government controlled and have good prices on traditional crafts and souvenirs. If you shop at street markets, be prepared to bargain over pricing. You will have to go several rounds of negotiations before settling on a price. The vendor will offer a high price and you should in turn say a low price. He expects (and wants) you to pay approximately half of his original asking price. But know that he can go lower. When you begin to barter, know how much you are willing to pay for something, and if you go through with the negotiations, make the purchase.

I am a big shopper, and I bought so much that our luggage weighed more going home than when we went. I had packed gifts and other belongings in several small boxes, which I then used to pack souvenirs for the return trip. Several of these were plastic shoeboxes. Nothing broke, but I'd suggest purchasing newspaper to wrap items in or taking a small amount of bubble wrap.

Souvenir items to look for:

- Carpets
- CD's—Folk music
- Chop (red ink, name stamp, made to order)
- Cloisonné—silverware, chopsticks, jewelry, pens, tie bars
- Clothing-Silk PJ'S, Dresses-Cheongsam)
- Combs
- Fans
- Jade (carvings, jewelry)

- Kites
- Musical instruments (tradtional-Chinese)
- Paintings
- Paper cuttings
- Pearls
- Porcelain
- Posters (don't forget mailer tubes to carry home)
- Silk—lipstick cases, makeup or glass cases, ties
- Tea sets (Enamel)

Chapter 20

Say Hello, Wave Goodbye

Finalizing the Adoption

The first thing that you will want to do after you arrive is meet your child. How soon you are able to do this will depend on the time of your arrival, whether you spend a few days in Beijing or Hong Kong before traveling to the province, or if you must first visit local government agencies prior to your meeting, and the adoption procedure in the province.

Provincial paperwork, paperwork completed in the province capital or nearest major city in the province that your daughter is from, issues you the final permission to adopt. The Adoption may be finalized at the same time/place or you may have to travel to the actual city that the orphanage is located. A Notary, an important government official in China, will finalize the adoption. Once he finalizes the adoption, it is final in both the both China and the United States.

If an adoption interview is conducted, it is possible that you may be asked questions concerning infertility, possible birth of biological children, why you want to adopt, how you plan to help preserve their heritage, child-care, finances, or home ownership. If you are a single parent, you may be asked similar questions. In addition, you may hear concerns about your ability to do this as a single parent, why you want to do this without a spouse, and infrequently, sexual orientation.

Besides the notary, you may meet other government representatives, the orphanage director or other members of the staff during this time. It is important to make a good first impression. Remember to dress accordingly. It is not necessary to dress up; skirts, dress's, a suit, coat and tie, or denim, no matter how dressy, is not appropriate attire when meeting with government officials. Sharp casual is the norm; khaki pants, a nice shirt.

Meeting Your Child

Children may have traveled by car or by bus to get to you. They may be tired or hungry. New sights, sounds and smells may cause disorientation. They may also have common medical conditions such as a common cold, respiratory infection, diaper rash, eczema, etc.

Once children arrive they are brought to their new parents and handed over. During the first meeting, your daughter may be scared or intimidated. She may be attached to a caregiver who is equally attached to her. It is also possible that she may never have spent any time around a male or that something may remind her of a previous negative experience. It is also possible that she is as overwhelmed as you may be.

When it's time to take custody of your daughter, it may be quite emotional. It can signify the completion of years of trying to build a family. While it is an emotional time for you, it can be emotional for orphanage staff, foster parents, or others who may have formed a strong attachment to your child. They may be equally torn between being happy for your child and being saddened by their loss.

Oftentimes the mood may be one of celebration. If possible, try to get a member of the staff or another family who may be traveling with you to record or take pictures of this first meeting.

Parents often want to undress and change their daughters' clothes as soon as possible. This is not the best idea unless clothes are obviously soiled. Wait a little while and give them time to adjust to their surroundings. When you do undress her be prepared, babies may be under nourished and as a whole, much smaller than U.S. babies. Most likely you will want this to be a special outfit, which will be a treasured keepsake. Save the clothes she was wearing as a memento. This may be her first disposable diaper and it may take her a bit to get used to.

You may receive a parting gift or memento of your child. If not, ask if there is an item of clothing or a favored possession that you can have. You may need to make a trade or purchase a replacement. For Callie, we have two beaded necklaces that were made by one of the orphanage workers.

During this first meeting, you will probably want to bring a small toy or treats to use as ice breakers. I took a small doll and a ball. Callie was shy at first, but after I pulled out the doll, we were in. Buy duplicates or triplicates of anything you consider special. You may want to buy one to give on the first meeting, and a second for a backup in case you lose the first and a third one could be for your memory box.

Early Days Together

Adoptive parents go through a similar pre-attachment process to their child that biological expectant parents experience. While adopted children may form attachments to caregivers, they rarely have the opportunity to experience pre-adoption attachment to adoptive parents.

Often families expect an immediate bond with their child. This may or may not happen. If it does not, this is not a cause to be alarmed but a normal part of the adjustment process. Children must learn to trust parents before forming attachments. While a bond may be instantaneous, secure attachment must take time to develop. Secure attachment can take several years.

Babies who are special needs and non-special needs, as well as biological children can have issues with attachment and developmental delays. For a child, residing in an orphanage increases their risks. One of the most positive features of China adoption is the age of the child at the time of adoption. The younger a child is at the time of adoption, the better, the less trauma that they may have experienced. They also have good caregivers.

Even so, during the early days together, many children may experience withdrawal, inconsolable crying, fear, shyness, avoidance, lack of interaction or expression, temper tantrums, or exhibit a fear of one parent. Babies bodies may feel a bit floppy if they have low muscle tone or muscle atrophy either from rickets or lying in a crib all day. They may appear listless, and may not smile or play except with their fingers. (Which may have been their only toy.) Thrashing their heads, refusing eye contact, sucking their thumbs or rocking are also common. Some children exhibit the opposite: they may be clingy and can not bear to be out of your sight.

Even very young babies experience grief and loss. Children who are being removed from everything they know, regardless of the positive or negative circumstance they were in, will experience trauma. Children who are in Foster Care will most likely have more pronounced grief.

Babies my refuse to eat, even if they are hungry. Try frequent small meals. Most likely they will want their food hot and sweet. What goes in must come out. If a baby is not eating, she may not go to the bathroom.

If the baby is difficult, not eating, etc., you must find out why. Consult with your guide, physician, adoption agency, adoptive parent mentor, etc. who may have some suggestions for you. If babies are sick they may need medical care. If not, they usually begin to perk up, and become more interactive within a few days.

This can be very frustrating time to parents, especially inexperienced, first time parents who may feel insecure in their new role. I *can not* stress enough how important pre-adoption education is. "Adoptive parents must accept the responsibility to seek and receive appropriate childcare education that is specifically related to adoption and other medical or special needs. Families must research available resources."

If you have not taken any pre-adoptive parenting classes, pre-adoption education, a course on post adoption issues, attachment, international adoption, etc. now is the time! The last thing you want to happen is find yourself in a hotel room in China wondering what to do next.

Attachment Parenting

Pre-adoption education, available resources, and how parents deal with post-adoption issues will significantly impact their daughter's long term, overall well being. Grief, trauma, attachment or other developmental issues all affect attachment.

Long term residual effects, which can negatively impact both children and families, include genealogy, race and identity, loss of birthparents, failure to attach and abandonment issues. All can leave adoptive parents questioning their parenting ability, especially if these feelings are not validated within their adoption community. Parenting a challenging child can be both stressful and exhausting. The most common symptoms of attachment issues are:

1. Sleep problems, night terrors, problems going to sleep
2. Demanding or clingy
3. Severe, prolonged anger, rage, or tantrums
4. Control issues
5. Difficulty with change, transition
6. Stiffens or dislikes being held, does not reciprocate hugs, wants to sit with back facing mother, prefers, playpen or crib.
7. Affectionate on own terms, cries or rages when held against her will. Indiscriminately friendly, prefers others over parents
8. Never comfortable, gets in and out of lap
9. Poor eye contact
10. Hyperactive, hyper-vigilant
11. Overly independent
12. Lifeless, rarely cries or smiles

Newly adopted children frequently exhibit some type of attachment issues during the transitional period. A child who has never sleep alone, or in the dark may be scared to go to sleep. A child who spent a year with a foster parent will grieve, just as a young child who has had to learn to feed or dress herself may be more independent than is age appropriate. This does not mean that they have or will develop attachment disorder; most will not, instead they can be a normal part of the process and may have issues that need to be resolved in order for the child to form a secure attachment.

Many children have developmental delays related to speech and language, or gross and fine motor skills. Most experience catch up growth, and quickly begin to make developmental strides but some may need outside services to help improve The changes you will see in your daughter, over the first two-three months will amaze you.

There are many things that you as a parent can do to help your child develop trust, improve stamina and cognitive development. In order to be most effective these should be geared toward emotional not chronological age. In some cases, it would be appropriate to parent younger babies the same or similar to how you would a newborn. Most of these will also help facilitate attachment and could be considered attachment or therapeutic parenting. You can begin immediately with your child.

Parenting Do's

- Mimic caregiver techniques and maintain routines when possible
- Set a structured routine, try to schedule activities at the same time everyday, your child will feel more secure
- Establish a bedtime routine, rock before bed, cuddle, etc.
- Gradually change diet
- Give them immediate response
- Reinforce eye contact-require eye contact when feeding, talking, ands rocking
- Control and limit settings
- Join self-soothing behavior (pick up and rock a rocking child)
- Comfort inconsolable crying, the urge will be not to but it is more beneficial to your child for you to hold them, pat their back, rub them, etc.
- Cuddle and hold them as much as possible. Don't worry about spoiling them

- Maximize skin contact
- Use baby massage techniques, for babies who are not use to touch, start slow
- Bathe or swim together
- Use same baby soap, shampoo, lotion, etc. as baby
- Use baby carriers in the face forward position
- Focus on Mom first as the primary caretaker and establish bond, then move on to others
- Limit exposure to others
- Ask a nurse or someone else to hold child during vaccinations
- Talk to babies, even if they are pre-verbal. Babies comprehend language before they begin to speak
- Say to them you are my good baby, my girl, etc.
- Smile at them
- Touch your child; pat, hug, place your hand on, kiss, etc.
- Play games—peek-a-boo, sing, clap, dance, make silly faces, roll a ball, etc.
- Join an adoption playgroup, playdates are important for socialization and to have a place where transracial families are the norm

For toddlers and older children
- Prepare your child for change
- Limit choices, parent chooses first them child can begin to choose between 2 choices
- Help identify their feelings and validate them
- Teach child to ask you first before doing
- Set limits, no means no
- Feed toddlers, even if they can feed themselves
- Feed each other treats
- Regress and bottle-feed toddlers
- Stay at home as long as possible before returning to work
- Try to communicate in child's native language for the first few months
- Don't force language

- Enroll school age children in school as quickly as possible—this will help language
- Play with dolls, especially baby dolls to mimic good parenting
- Play with bubbles, books, music, blocks, color, draw, and playdough
- Play hide and seek, do not leave if child is distressed or jump out if they are scared
- Ride bicycle, tricycle, wagon rides
- Take trips to the park or zoo
- Hold hands when walking together
- Give Eskimo or butterfly kisses
- Use natural consequences for discipline
- Use physical exercise for consequences
- Have them do chores, this teaches responsibility and helps build self-esteem, they can do extra as a consequence
- Have them earn and loose privileges
- Use time in, not time outs

Don'ts
- No corporal punishment for traumatized kids
- Do not let babies "cry it out." Comfort crying
- Do not use baby carrier to sit baby in, hold them instead
- Do not allow the child to be the center of attention
- Do not put child in daycare, immediately or use nanny, babysitters, etc.
- Do not enroll older children in English as a Second Language class
- Do not let them over indulge in junk foods, especially sweets, require them to eat healthy
- Do not over stimulate child, no trips to the mall, Disney World, etc.
- Limit television, choose non-violent, non-aggressive programs such as educational television or Disney

Traveling With Your Child

Once your adoption has been finalized, your paperwork notarized, and you have obtained your daughter's Chinese passport, you will then travel from the province to Guangzhou to complete the last leg of your journey. In Guangzhou, you will complete the immigration paperwork at the U.S. Embassy. Prior to the embassy appointment, your daughter will be required to have a medical exam. After the Embassy appointment, (usually the next day) you will recive your child's U.S visa and you may begin your trip home.

When preparing to travel home with your daughter, it may feel like the climax of your trip, but in fact the real adventure is just beginning. Most likely, your child has never ridden in a car, train, or plane. Since you have no idea if she is susceptible to motion sickness (or sensitive to new foods, as in our case), you may want to have an airsick bag on hand for emergencies.

Your daughter may have never been in a car seat or any type of seating where she was restrained for a short period—much less for an extended time. Children two and older must have their own airplane seat. If you are planning on using a car seat, you may want to try to help her become accustomed to sitting in it before you board the plane.

Changes in air pressure for young children who have had frequent ear infections can be painful. It is not uncommon to have crying babies on return flights, and they may be equally uncomfortable with their new surroundings and new parents.

If you are lucky, your child will sleep a large portion of your trip. Traveling as direct as possible will help relieve some of the fatigue. When you are traveling during your daughter's active time of day, you may find that you have to take walks up and down the aisles or try to hold her in your lap. For small toddlers, you may want to consider using a lap belt attachment during the flight.

To help pass the time, you should be armed with a variety of toys or treats for your toddler. A small child's backpack is a great way to carry these, and it could be carried within your diaper bag or other carry on luggage.

Diaper bags should have a pocket for bottles, exterior pockets and or organizer, a bag liner which can be easily cleaned, adjustable straps, laundry bag, changing pad, and insulated bottle bag. Many people opt to use backpacks because they are easy to carry, and have great compartments to put stuff in.

Carry on essentials: Diaper bag or backpack

- Bibs (disposable)
- Blanket

- Burp cloth (2)
- Change of clothes
- Changing pad
- Diapers
- Formula (and everything you need to prepare it)
- Insulated bottle bag
- Medications (any she is taking or may need)
- Pacifier with leash
- Sippy cups or bottles
- Small Toys
- Snacks
- Sweater

For older toddlers and young children, try a small child's backpack that they can carry themselves. Most likely they will think this is really "cool." Fill with lots of things to do: coloring books, crayons, light weight books, doll and accessories, etc. (Avoid battery operated musical toys—they get tiresome after a long flight, plus if the battery dies from being used repeatedly you will be in trouble if you do not have a back up.)

Also include your child's basics either in her or your backpack: pull-ups, sippy cup or other utensils, and a change of clothes. (two for small children) Don't forget to pack a change of clothes for each parent. At the very least, parents of small children should pack an extra shirt.

Chapter 21

Home Sweet Home

Some people have huge arrival parties at the airport, while others are simply greeted by immediate family. Adoptive families have varying travel experiences. Families may have great trips that might include sightseeing and a pleasant stay while others may have endured less desirable conditions, or had various other problems. On the return trip home, some families may have minimized travel time by flying more direct routes while others may have traveled nonstop for thirty or more hours—possibly with an angry, screaming or sick baby in tow.

Travel, fatigue, food- or waterborne illnesses and the completion of the adoption process can all be overwhelming for new parents. Most likely, you will want to go home, eat, and sleep.

Before we had even stopped coasting down the runway, my husband spotted Grandma armed with a giant Winnie the Pooh and the rest of the grandparents plastered against the windows of the terminal.

Our plane arrived around lunchtime, and our parents drove us home where they had stocked our refrigerator and prepared lunch. We ate lunch and they were thrilled to visit with Callie, their first grandchild.

We were equally thrilled when they left a short time later so we could nap. Because your new arrival may have trouble adjusting to the time change or changes in his environment, it may be necessary to make prior arrangements with friends or family who can help while you are catching up on much needed rest and recuperation.

Meeting the New Arrival

Once friends and family learn that you are home, your phone will probably be ringing off the hook with well-wishers who want to come and visit. It is best to forewarn them of your plans.

You may want to have a nesting period and minimize outside contact. You need to establish yourself as the primary caretaker and may find it necessary to educate others regarding feeding, hugging, picking up or other physical contact with your daughter.

Start slowly by inviting a small intimate group of friends over. Avoid curiosity seekers or gossipmongers. Large groups or noise may overwhelm your daughter. By inviting too many people over at once, the focus shifts from meeting the new addition to socializing between guests. The last thing you want to worry about is cooking, cleaning, or entertaining.

Many people who visit you and your daughter will want to bring a present, even if they attended a baby shower. Try to limit the amount of gifts your daughter is given. If you are swamped with gifts, try to tuck some away for future use.

Parenting

After you arrive home, you will discover that your work has only just begun. Each family member will need time to become acquainted with one another. You will have to establish new routines, and it will take time to figure out what your daughter's needs are. During this time, both you and your daughter may experience frustration, anger, or anxiety.

During early days together, sleep when the baby sleeps. Let housework go or hire a cleaning person. If someone offers help, take them up on it. If you need help, don't be afraid to ask. Spend quality time getting to know your daughter. Join a mom's group or an adoption support group.

Many children experience grief or fear after leaving their old home, regardless of what the conditions may have been. Your daughter may be somewhat depressed or angry that you have taken her away from familiar surroundings, her caretakers, or other children. She may throw temper tantrums, cry, or otherwise act out her frustration. This frustration may be aimed at her primary caretaker, and it is not uncommon for children to show a preference for one parent over another.

Relationships with friends will change, and you may suddenly find yourself "on the outside looking in." This may be especially true if you have many childless friends. You will lose much of your ability to be spontaneous, and you may not be able to participate in social activities if you receive little advance notice. Simple things such as running to the grocery store may require scheduling and preparation, which could include finding a sitter, scheduling around naps, or packing a diaper bag.

If one parent is staying at home while the other returns to work, his or her lifestyle may change more significantly. The working parent may have a harder time adjusting to lifestyle changes in his or her nonworking hours because they have resumed a normal work schedule.

A working parent may not witness much of the child's normal routine or behavior and might be unaware of how any changes may affect the child. For example, this parent may not know that at 10:30, Susie gets a snack and that when she is hungry, she gets tired and irritable. The parent may assume that since it is only an hour and a half to lunchtime that she doesn't need a snack and can wait until then and eat.

In another scenario, the parent may think that snacks are treats and may decide that because Susie is grumpy or misbehaving that she can't have a treat. In both cases, hunger and the need to eat cause Susie's behavior. Instead of fixing the problem, it is aggravated.

Children need structure, and a working parent who is home all day on the weekends can throw a monkey wrench into the mix. One parent may not appreciate having to defer to the other parent's child-care expertise. Moreover, the child may ignore primary caretaker when the other parent is present. Single parents need a strong support system, which may include friends and family who have the same value system and can help fill in as needed.

Parents or caregivers often have different ideas about the importance of schedules as well as discipline and other parenting skills. These differences should be discussed before the adoption takes place because they can cause disagreements. Adoptive families must work together to fulfill their parenting responsibilities. At the same time, parents must also be allowed time to become parents. It may not be easy, but you will be able to find balance.

Post-Adoption Depression

Postpartum depression has long been attributed to changes in hormone levels after birth. However, a significant portion of adoptive parents report experiencing post-adoption depression (PAD). This often unrecognized form of depression might be unknown to health-care workers and adoption professionals.

The symptoms are the same as those for most forms of depression. They may include fatigue, irritability, loss of appetite, sadness, and a general sense of being overwhelmed. Individuals with a history of depression or families who have experienced failed adoptions or the loss of a referral may be at higher risk for PAD and may be more likely to experience it.

Finalizing an adoption is an emotional climax to perhaps years of trying to build a family. The stress of the process may be replaced by the new stress of caring for your child. PAD may be affected by unresolved infertility issues, physical demands of your child, changes in peer relationships, fear of legal issues arising with the adoption, or health problems (yours or your child's).

These feelings are not uncommon and will pass. However, because PAD can negatively affect attachment and bonding, it is important to seek help as necessary, which may include professional aid or friends and family who can help. Your needs and available resources will the level of help you seek.

Health Care

If you have not pre-registered your child for health-care coverage, you need to do so immediately. If you have group health-care coverage, you have only thirty days from the date the adoption was completed to enroll your child for health insurance. You should follow up and make sure that your human resources representatives have completed the enrollment and remind them of the time limitation.

Denial of coverage or classifying an adopted child as having a pre-existing condition is not allowed by group health coverage under the Health Insurance and Portability and Accountability Act of 1996. Families who are independent business owners or those who work for a small company and are not covered by a group insurance plan are not covered by this act and need to know their options. You should research your insurance policy and provisions because there are some exceptions. Always document your conversation and note the name of the person you spoke with.

Readoption

Readoption usually means that a local court or judge will review the documentation of your foreign adoption and issue a new, U.S. adoption decree. Whether or not this is necessary will be determined by state law, the type of Visa that your child enters the U.S. on and sometimes the country from which you adopt. If your state requires a readoption, it is because it either does not recognize the finalization of an adoption by a foreign country or provide the same rights an adopted child. The regulations and procedure will vary by state.

For China, readoption is not usually necessary, unless only one parent travels and your child enters the U.S. on a IR4 Visa. If both parents travel then an IR-3 is issued. If your child receives an IR-3 Visa then she is an automatic citizen when she enters the United States. An IR-3 does not require families to do a re-adoption but many people choose to. Most adoption attorneys usually recommend readoption. A readoption will ensure that your child has all rights under U.S. law and in every state in the U.S. These laws can effect social security benefits and inheritance.

If only one parent traveled to China to complete the adoption, meaning that only one parent saw the child before the adoption proceedings, then the child is issued an IR-4 Visa. This means that when your child enters the country she will not be an automatic U.S. citizen but a permanent resident. You must apply for citizenship with the United States Citizenship and Immigration Services. However; in order to meet the requirements for citizenship, you must first complete a readoption.

Should you lose your original, Chinese issued birth certificate, it would be almost impossible to replace. Further complicating the use of the Chinese birth certificate is that it written in Chinese instead of English. In most cases your child will be issued a state birth certificate when you go through the readoption process. From that point forward should she need one, it can be re-ordered from the state office of vital statistics.

A legal name change may also be part of the re-adoption process. Should you decide to change your child's name, or if the child's U.S. visa or immigration documents are in her Chinese name that may be a problem for some USCIS and Social Security offices who may refuse to issue documents in her American name.

The readoption process usually consist of an application process, gathering of documentation, and a family court hearing in which an attorney and a guardian ad litem may be required. The court hearing is more a formality than an actual hearing. Most judges enjoy the celebratory mood of these hearings and many families use this as an opportunity for further celebration.

In some States it may be possible to complete a domestication of a foreign adoption as opposed to a readoption. In most cases the legal rights stated in each of the two processes are similar and most issue birth certificates. The primary difference is that in domestication an attorney or a court hearing may not be necessary. If this is the case it may be less expensive than a readoption. You should consulate an adoption or immigration attorney within you state to help you determine what your state requirements are and which might be best for you.

U.S. Passport

A passport is a travel document that verifies the identity and nationality of the bearer. It is internationally recognized and U.S. citizens are required to have a valid U.S. passport when entering and leaveing most foreign countries. All children regardless of age must have their own passport.

To obtain a passport for the first time, the child must first be a U.S. Citizen. Proof of citizenship is not a requirement to obtain a passport and your child and she does not need to wait until she receives the certificate of citizenship from the USCIS before obtaining a passport. Many adoption professionals recommend families apply for passports as soon as possible in order to establish proof of citizenship.

If your daughter came home on an IR-3 visa, she qualified for automatic citizenship and the foreign adoption is considered final. If she traveled on an IR-4 visa, families must complete a readoption in the U.S. before automatic citizenship applies and you can submit a passport application.

If the child's American name is not on the child's foreign paperwork and if you have completed either a readoption or legal change of name in the U.S., the passport will be issued in the child's foreign name.

The U.S. Department of State requires all minors (under the age of 14) applying for U.S. passports to personally appear at the passport office. Most passport offices require appointments. Both parents must appear together with the child at a passport acceptance facility located throughout the United States.

If both parents can not appear, one parent may appear, sign, and submit second parent's notarized statement of consent authorizing passport issuance for the child. (A notarized Form DS-3053, Statement of Consent: Issuance of a Passport to a Minor Under Age 14) You will need the following documents:

- Passport Application Form DS-11
- Evidence of the child's relationship to a U.S. citizen parent-A certified copy of the final adoption decree with adoptive parents names
- The child's foreign passport with the USCIS's I-551 stamp or the child's resident alien card
- Proof of parent's valid identification and citizenship
- 2 identical passport pictures
- Passport application fee, security surcharge, and execution fee

For additional Passport information see U.S. Department of State at: http://travel.state.gov/passport/passport_1738.html or call the National Passport Information Center, Toll-free: 1-877-487-2778

Certificates of Citizenship

The Child Citizenship Act, effective February 27, 2001, amends the Immigration and Nationality Act to provide U.S. citizenship to include adopted children of U.S. citizens. Citizenship is automatic to adopted children who enter the U.S. on an IR-3 visa.

The Child Citizenship Act Program became effective January 20, 2004. Under this program, Certificates of Citizenship will be automatically provided, at no extra charge. Children will no longer be issued a Permanent Alien Resident Card and should receive their Certificates of Citizenship within 45 days of entry into the United States. Exceptions to this are:

1. Children over 14 years of age are required to take the oath of allegiance before the certificate of citizenship is issued.

2. Children who entered the U.S. on an IR-4 visa, must finalize their adoption in the U.S. through re-adoption before they are eligible to apply for a certificate of citizenship. To receive a Certificate of Citizenship, submit the Form N-600, Application for Certificate of Citizenship. Submit the application to your USCIS field office.

3. If you and your child permanently reside abroad, your child does not qualify for automatic citizenship. You can apply for citizenship for your child by filing form N-600K

For more information about the Child Citizenship Act, procedures and forms see: www.uscis.gov/graphics/citizenship/index.htm

Obtaining a Social Security Number

Once you have arrived home, you will need to apply for a Social Security number for your daughter. You need this in order to claim your child as a dependent on your income tax return or possibly open a bank account, buy savings bonds, obtain medical coverage for the child or apply for government services for the child.

To find your nearest Social Security office or to apply for a Social Security number for your child, you need to complete Form SS-5 which is available for download from the Social Security Administration see http://www.ssa.gov. You will need to submit evidence of:

Proof of Child's Age

- Child's birth certificate or adoption decree as evidence of your child's date of birth.
- Child's passport, or documentation issued to your child by the U.S. Immigration and Naturalization Service.

Proof of Identity

A recently issued document establishing you and your child's continued existence: a document with name as well as age, date of birth, parents' names. A Child's Proof of identity may include adoption records and USCIS documents. Parents proof of identity, including, Driver's License, Passport, Marriage or Divorce Record. A birth certificate can not be used as an identity document.

U.S. Citizenship/Lawful Alien Status

If your child has a Certificate of Citizenship or a U.S. passport you should submit this as proof of citizenship. Even if you do not have proof of your child's citizenship, the Social Security Administration can still assign a number based on the documentation issued to your child by the Immigration and Naturalization Service upon arrival in the U.S. When you receive documentation of your child's citizenship, bring it to your local Social Security _ and they will update your child's record. Your child will not be penalized and their Social Security number will not change.

Some Social Security Offices will not issue Social Security Number without proof of citizenship in order to issue a social security number. If you not yet received your Certificate of Citizenship, then your adoption agency may be able to write a letter explaining the situation. In most cases, the Social Security office will issue a number with this letter in hand.

All documents need to be originals or copies certified by the issuing custodian of the record. Notarized photocopies of documents are not accepted. Documents should be returned to you. Once all necessary documents have been sent in, it should take about two weeks to receive your child's Social Security card.

Fielding Adoption Questions

Anyone who knows you are in the adoption process or meets your new child will have plenty of personal questions or comments. These questions will be asked regardless of your child's presence, age, and comprehension level, and without consideration of his or her feelings.

Disclose only the information you wish to and answer only those questions you are comfortable with. If you feel that questions are inappropriate, do not answer. Inappropriate questions may include what happened to her real parents, what do you know about her real parents, how much did it (the adoption) or she (your daughter) cost, why was she in an orphanage? Chinese adoptive parents may also receive comments about the country of China, human rights, child abandonment or trade agreements.

You will soon learn to tell the difference between people who are generally interested in adoption and those who are curiosity seekers or looking for a juicy story. One option to fielding adoption questions is to respond, "If you are interested in adoption, call me and I would be happy to talk to you about it or send you some information." If you are being pushed for answers, asking, "Why do you want to know?" may help, and for those who are truly obnoxious, there is always the "that's none of your business" or "this is a private family matter" answer.

You have probably already been told countless negative adoption stories about medical problems, disrupted adoptions, or stories about people who get pregnant after they adopt. Unfortunately, these stories do not stop once you have completed your adoption.

Negative stereotypes regarding adoptive children include the belief that there must be something wrong with the child, that she was abandoned, abused, or neglected, or that you are a great and courageous person who went halfway around the world to give this child a home and she must be eternally grateful because you "saved her."

Sometimes well-meaning individuals will not understand an adoptive family's sensitivity to negative adoption language, and it is our added responsibly to help teach positive adoption language. I recently spoke to an adult adoptee who referred to his birth mom as his "real" mom. On another occasion, I was annoyed enough to ask the pediatrician's office if my child was considered unnatural since the question was stated, "Is this your natural child?" as opposed to using the term birth child or biological.

Preparing for questions in advance will help alleviate some of the awkwardness that you may feel when faced with confrontation. Just when you think you may have heard it all, you will be surprised by an unexpected question. Having answers ready will help show your child how to handle these situations as she takes over the responsibility and decides when and what to tell people about her adoption. When she chooses to open this door, she will inevitably find that she will be in the position of fielding such questions.

Transracial Adoption

Some people may not understand your desire to adopt transracially, and you may experience unexpected prejudices. Even those you know and love may surprise you. You will be asked many personal questions that may be inappropriate. When you are with your child, you may experience rude stares or unnecessary comments from strangers.

People may ask you if this is your child or may assume that you are babysitting or that your spouse is of the same race as your child. You will also get ridiculous questions such as will your child speak Chinese (even if she is a baby who cannot talk) or if is she a member of the Communist party.

Families who adopt transracially may find that they receive criticism within their own community and on rare occasions, from those who are native to their child's birth country. Sometimes, friends or relatives who were less than thrilled at the prospect of your adoption may be even more standoffish once you are home.

On the opposite end of the spectrum, your child may be treated as a novelty, and singled out because of her uniqueness. Constantly being the center of attention can adversely affect the development of personal identity and cause her to develop a sense of entitlement.

Most adoptive children whether adopted by parents of the same or different race must be equipped to deal with the adoption issues of grief, loss abandonment, When families decide on a transracial adoption, they add another layer of the already complex issue of adoption. Families not only have to address adoption issues but race and adoption.

Adoptive parents have the added responsibility of helping teach children cultural competency, to be able to able to identify with both cultures, and to recognize the importance of culture to personal identity and adjustment. As part of this process children will have to explore their origins, and what it means to be part of a family.

In addition, parents must teach their children about racial issues without every having experienced prejudice based on race and cultural stereotypes. This can be challenging for parents who may have to actively seek out specific learning opportunities and assistance in their area.

Suggested reading: *Intercountry Adoption From China, Examining Cultural Heritage and Other Post Adoption Issues* by Jay W. Rojewski and Jacy L. Rojewski, and *Inside Transracial Adoption* by Beth Hall and Gail Steinberg

Toddlers as young as age three start to recognize differences in physical characteristics and begin to ask questions about. Some will want to change their features while others start to understand the values that society places on them. They may begin to feel what it is like to be a minority. By age five or six they probably have experienced their first racial slur or have had someone make "Chinese eyes" to them.

As children reach adolescence they begin to understand adoption issues. They develop a peer group where adoption and race are socially acceptable. They begin to explore and think about race and will need for you to discuss adoption with them, as is age appropriate.

Teenagers explore their identity. They may experience more prejudice. A neighbor or family friend who has always been accepting may suddenly be opposed to your daughter dating thier son. Prejudice and racism may come from people they know or do not know.

The adoption community is important to your daughter. As members of an adoptive family group, your family will be the norm. It is important to nurture your daughters need to have a "sense of belonging" Finding balance is key. Each child is different and you must follow her lead. Her needs will change over time.

Post-Adoption Support

With more than 100,000 children adopted annually by United States citizens, adoptive families everywhere are banning together to find ways to promote adoption awareness and advocacy. Flexing their collective muscles, adoptive families have had offensive TV and radio spots pulled, laws changed that fail to properly address adoption fraud or recognize adoptive families rights, and effectively shut down adoption agencies that are not in compliance with state regulations.

But it's not just about fighting the good fight; many adoptive families do a great deal of humanitarian work as well. Whether it's shoe collection drives for groups like *Shoes for Orphan Souls* or small business owner's like Kari Hunt or Ruth Ellen Heaton of *A Mother's Charm* who donate a portion of thier proceeds to charity, adoptive families find many ways to give back to the community.

One of the ways adoptive families do this is to facilitate and participate in adoption support groups. Many serve as mentors to families who are just beginning the adoption process, adopting through the same agency or from the same country. Adoptive families interact with one another on an almost daily basis through participation in a variety of local or internet advocacy or support organizations and adoption agency sponsored activities.

Many adoption agencies have Parents in Progress groups and offer a variety of post-adoptive family events, summer camps, or other services for their clients. You may want to consider contacting your local Chapter of Families with Children from China for recommendations on non-agency-affiliated adoption support groups or playgroups in your area. Activities range from adoption playgroups—culture camps—mom's night out—providing pre-adoption information and related family activities.

You may also find a large spectrum of adoption support and advocacy organizations on the Internet. These include A-Parent-China and Waiting Children China. Some may be country-specific while others may be open to all adoptive families living within a geographical region.

The camaraderie one can find within adoption support organizations is similar to that in any typical family or child oriented organization, with the added benefits of meeting the unique needs of adoptive families. Often new parents may have questions that only adoptive families can answer. At times this exchange of information may be critical for new adoptive families or families in crisis.

Because each child comes equipped with his own unique set of circumstances even seasoned parents may benefit from this exchange of information. Discussions on how to fund an adoption, adoption legislation, medical and educational resources, cultural events, and adoption travel are the norm.

Support group participation can be especially important for families who adopted through an out of state adoption agency. Finding local resources for your child can be frustrating and time consuming. Having contacts who have "been their and done that", can help navigate the complex process of accessing services through early intervention programs, preschool services, or the special educational system and recommend a pediatrician who is experienced with internationally adopted children or more specialized medical services.

One of the most positive benefits of a family based or child centered support organization is that children can meet and interact with other adopted children. Children, who are adopted as toddlers and know their own adoption story, as is age appropriate, may have a more secure comfort level with how families are formed. Older children who experience support from adopted peers often have a better understanding of the complexity of adoption as it is related to race, cultural heritage, or the social-economic circumstances of birthparents or birth country.

While we may take this for granted now, it may be more important as your child grows and matures. It is also important for Chinese children to know that children are adopted from other countries besides China and other Asian countries.

And let's not forget about the social and emotional support provided by adoption support groups. Being a parent is never easy, being an adoptive parent may be even harder. Meeting the day to day parenting needs required by a child who may have developmental delays, special needs, or is simply strong willed, can exhaust even the most energetic of parents. Having someone to listen to you while you moan and complain or proudly boast accomplishments, which might be seen as minor to others—someone who truly understands—can be very therapeutic.

For adoption support groups there are more reasons to get together than secret recipes for Borscht. Families of Chinese children celebrate Chinese New Year while Russian born children are taught folk tales of Baba Yaga. There is International Women's Day, the Harvest Moon Festival, and Name Days: each one a reason to celebrate adoption, the diversity of the family, and to promote a better understanding of the uniqueness of adoptive families. While it is this uniqueness that brings them together, it is the similarities that bind adoptive families together.

Ways to Celebrate Adoption

1. Learn Mandarin Chinese and teach basics: counting to ten, basic conversational skills to your children.

2. Listen to and teach your children to appreciate traditional Chinese instrumental or folk music.

3. Attend local Cultural events, such as Chinese New Years Celebrations.

4. Find someone who is Chinese that has a child close to your child's age, or identify an adult to serve as a mentor or role model for your child.

5. Teach your child to locate China, and the province they were born in on a globe, or map.

6. Celebrate Chinese Holidays or choose a Chinese tradition or custom to incorporate into your family.

7. Learn to cook Chinese, order take out, or dine at a Chinese restaurant.

8. Practice making your own Chinese craft such as lantern making or learn origami.

9. Read books that provide positive role models, read Chinese folk tales.

10. Play a game or other activity that is frequently played by Chinese children.

11. Attend adoption agency events or activities sponsored by local adoption support groups.

12. Sponsor a project, collection, shoe drive, etc., which will benefit waiting Chinese children.

Visitation, and Post-Placement

The CCAA requires two post-placement reports after the completion of an adoption. These are due 6 months and one year after the adoption is completed. Most adoption agencies wish to fulfill this obligation and will contact the family prior to when post-placements are due.

If you had a less-than-ideal adoption process and have discontinued the relationship with your agency, you may have to be creative to fulfill this obligation. It may be necessary to schedule post-placements and deal directly with your social worker, another facilitator, the orphanage director, the Chinese Consulate, or other adoptive families. It is imperative that adoptive parents comply with the terms of adoption and take responsibility for the completion of these reports.

Failure to complete post-placement reports ultimately results in more regulations and more difficulty in the completion of adoptions for other families who follow in your footsteps. Failing to provide post-placements may also help perpetuate unfounded rumors involving the treatment of adopted children. This can and does result in investigations and the suspension of adoptions.

Homeland Visits

Often times as children grow, their families travel to their birth country to visit. Children should be approximately seven to ten-years old when they make their first trip, (Unless traveling with family to complete a second adoption). You will find child-centric, family focused travel programs that include learning the language, Chinese culture, history, sightseeing and volunteer opportunities.

This is a great opportunity for your child to see and learn first hand what they have only heard, read, or dreamed, about. China becomes a tangible reality that they can see, feel and touch. It is important for children to identify positively with their homeland. Travel to China will help them gain knowledge of core Chinese values, socially accepted behavior and identify with people of their own race.

While most Homeland visits, include a trip to visit your child's orphanage, you will need to decide if this is age appropriate and in the best interest of your child. In some cases children who were in Foster Care may be able to visit their foster families. Families who participate must be prepared to explore adoption issues before, during and after their journey.

Staying in Contact

Besides completing post-placement reports, we regularly send updates about Callie to the orphanage. If you are as fortunate to have had an excellent staff, interpreter, guide, etc. during your adoption travel, you may wish to remain in contact with them. In addition, you may want to send updates to your daughter's foster parents or other caretakers who are genuinely interested in your daughter's well being.

You should get any addresses or phone numbers while you are with them. Many times adoption agencies may not have or be authorized to release this information. I cannot think of a better legacy for your child than establishing a permanent relationship with those who helped you with your adoption.

Epilogue

The long wait, preparing the nursery, packing for your trip, none of these things can ever truly prepare you for this trip of a lifetime. From the moment you board the plane and for many years to come your life will be forever changed by the wondrous miracle of adoption, the Chinese people, and of course your daughter.

No words can describe the overwhelming joy the first time you see your child, the first smile, or the first time she says Mommy. These along with the first spontaneous, hug, kiss, or gift have the power to heal the memories of years of infertility, the loss of a child or numerous, sleepless nights anticipating the arrival of your daughter.

"A journey of a thousand miles begins with one step", says the Chinese Proverb. This single step leads us to the Chinese philosophy of Yin and Yang and applies it to adoption. The positive and the negative: the opposite of one another, that must coexist in order to maintain harmony and balance. Joy and sorrow, abandoned and adopted, barren and fruitful: all forever entangled in the red thread.

It is our destiny.

Denise Harris Hoppenhauer

Resources

Adoption Resources

Adoption Coalition for Education and Support (ACES)
Adoptive family resource in South Carolina, Collaborates with all members of the adoption triad to provide families with pre-and post adoption education and support.
www.ACESKIDS.org

Adopting.com
Information resource for prospective parent information and parenting information
www.adopting.com

Adoption.com
Great resource for all types of adoption information
www.adoption.com

Adoption Guides
Licensed in North Carolina and South Carolina, Adoption Guides works with all citizens of the United States, including Americans living abroad, who wish to adopt.
www.adoptionguides.org

Adoption Learning Partners
Online Adoption Education courses
www.adoptionlearningpartners.org

Adoption Today
Bimonthly magazine about adoption
www.adoptinfo.net
(888) 924-6736

Adoptive Families magazine
Bimonthly adoptive parent magazine; publishers of the annual *Adoption Guide*
www.AdoptiveFamiliesMagazine.com
(646) 366-0830

The American Adoption Congress (AAC)
Provides help with all areas of adoption
P.O. Box 42730
Washington, D.C. 20015
(202) 483-3399
www.americanadoptioncongress.org

The Assistant Stork
Document facilitation, courier service
www.asststork.com

*Attach-China International
Provides post-adoption educational information for parents of children adopted from China, specifically about attachment, Reactive Attachment Disorder and Post Traumatic Stress Disorder.
www.attach-china.org

Beacon House Adoption Services
A fully licensed 501(c)(3), non profit, charitable child placing agency offering international adoption, home study and post placement services.

Caring Hands Services Inc.
Washington, D.C. based document authentication service.
http://www.caring-hands-service.com/index.htm

China Adoption Resources
A resource guide to adopting from China
www.chinaadoptionresources.com

China Connection
Include National Newsletter for China Adoptive Parents
www.chinaconnectiononline.com

Comeunity
Provides adoptive resources including book reviews, medical and health information, special-needs adoption, and more
www.comeunity.com

The Evan B. Donaldson Adoption Institute
Nonprofit organization whose mission is to improve adoption; home of the "Adoption Institute Newsletter"
www.adoptioninstitute.org

*Families with Children from China (FCC)
Support organization for families who have adopted from China and prospective adoptive parents. Includes many resources for adoptive families.
www.fwcc.org

Families with Children from Vietnam
www.fcvn.org

Half the Sky Foundation
Provides early education and nurture for almost 3000 orphans in China
www.halfthesky.org

Joint Council on International Children's Services
Affiliation of inter-country adoption agencies; promotes ethical practice and child welfare services
www.jcics.org

Journey to Me
On-line adoption journal for your adoption journey.
www.journeytome.com

Korean Adoption
www.adoptkorea.com

Legal-Eaze
International Adoption Document and Authentication Specialists
www.legaleaze.com

Love Without Boundaries.com
Provides medical, nutritional, educational and Foster Care assistance to waiting children in China.
www.lovewithoutboundaries.com

National Adoption Information Clearinghouse
Comprehensive resource on all aspects of adoption
330 C St. SW
Washington D.C., 20447
www.naic.af.hhs.gov/index.cfm

National Council for Single Adoptive Parents
P.O. Box 55
Wharton, NJ 07885
www.adopting.org/ncsap.html

North American Council on Adoptable Children
Advocates for waiting children, adoption support groups, and subsidies
970 Raymond Avenue, Suite 106
St. Paul, MN 55114-1149
(651) 644-3036
www.nacac.org

Older Child Adoption On-line Magazine
For older-child adoptive families or those who are adopting an older child; practical insights into older child adoption
www.olderchildadoption.com

OrphanDoctor.com
Adoption and medical resources for internationally adopted children, including medical research and definitions
www.orphandoctor.com

*Our Chinese Daughters Foundation
Non-profit foundation, supports families with Chinese children, homeland tours, Adoption, orphan support projects, education, newsletters, cultural events and programs and more.
www.OCDF.org

Parent Network for the Post-Institutionalized Child
For parents of children who are adopted internationally
www.pnpic.org

Project Katherine
Non-profit organization created to assist families with post institutional children, typically children adopted internationally
www.projectkatherine.org

Rainbow Kids International
International adoption publication
www.rainbowkids.com

Resolve—The National Infertility Association
Infertility support, local chapter information
www.resolve.org

Stars of David Int'l, Inc.
Information and support network for Jewish adoptive families
www.starsofdavid.org

Travel China Guide
Largest online China travel agency
www.travelchinaguide.com

Travel Protectors
Specializing in international travel insurance
www.travelprotectors.com

The Welcome Garden
Adoption resource created to encourage adoption, Home of the Adoption journal, Waiting children, news, and more.
www.Welcomegarden.com

* Favorite China adoption sites

Yahoo Groups

A-Parents-China
The largest adoption list with over 7,000 members, pre- and post adoptive families.
http://groups.yahoo.com/group/a-parents-china

Adopt Older Kids China (AOK)
htpp://groups.yahoo.com/group/Adopt-Older-Kids-China

Adopting From Cambodia
htpp://groups.yahoo.com/group/Cambodiandoptions

Post Adopt China
htpp://groups.yahoo.com/group/post-adopt-china

Raising China Children
Families of preschool and school age kids
htpp://groups.yahoo.com/group/rasingchinachildren

Waiting Children China
Parents adopting waiting children (special needs)
htpp://groups.yahoo.com/group/waitngchildrenchina

Child Advocacy, State and Federal Agencies

Centers for Disease Control
Provides information on vaccinations and safe food and water when traveling
www.cdc.org

Hague Adoption Standards Project
Draft standards to accredit agencies that provide international adoption services per guidelines to implement the Hague Treaty on Intercountry Adoption
www.hagueregs.org

U.S. Department of State
Official information on international adoption law and USCIS requirements.
U.S. embassies and other diplomatic missions
www.travel.state.gov/family/adoption/adoption_485.html

United States Citizenship and Immigration Services
www.USCIS.gov

Physicians

Dr. Jane Aronson
International Pediatric Health Services, PLLC
151 East 62nd St., Suite 1A
New York, NY 10021
(212) 207-6666
Fax (212) 207-6665
www.orphandoctor.com
E-mail orphandoctor@aol.com

Dr. Julie Bledsoe
The Center for Adoption Medicine, University of Washington, Pediatric Care Unit
4245 Roosevelt Way, NE
Seattle, WA, 98105
206-598-3006

Dr, Ira J. Chasnoff
Children's Research Triangle
180 N. Michigan Ave., Suite 700
Chicago, IL, 60601
www.childstudy.org
312-726-4011

Dr. Alla Gordina
Global Pediatrics,
International Adoption Medical Support Services
www.GlobalPediatrics.net
732-432-7777

Dr. Dana Johnson
International Adoption Clinic
University of Minnesota
420 Delaware St. SE
Minneapolis, MN 55455
(612) 624-1164

Angela LaRosa
Andrea Summer
International Adoption Clinic at the Medical University of South Carolina-Charleston, Children's Hospital
135 Rutledge Ave.
P.O. Box 250561
Charleston, SC 29425
843-876-8512.

Dr. Laurie Miller
International Adoption Clinic
750 Washington, St., NEMC 286
Boston, MA 02111
617-636-8121

Services and Support

Adoption Medical News
Information about adoption and health
www.adoptionmedicalnews.com

The American Academy of Allergy, Asthma, and Immunology
611 E. Wells St.
Milwaukee, WI 53202
(800) 822-2762
www.aaai.org

American Academy of Pediatrics
Has provisional sections on adoption and foster care; includes medical recommendations for adopted children
www.aap.org/sections/adoption/resources.htm

Center for Cognitive Developmental Assessment and Remediation
Cognitive, language, behavioral, and educational assessment for internationally
adopted children; Dr. Boris Gindis
www.bgcenter.com

CHADD-Children and Adults with Attention Disorders
Nonprofit organization serving individuals with attention deficit/hyperactivity
disorder
www.chadd.org

Children Unlimited
Attachment, adoption and family preservation, respite, mediation, and
education
www.children-unlimited.org

Institute for Attachment and Child Development
www.instituteforattachment.org

March of Dimes Birth Defects Foundation
Community Services Department
1275 Mamaroneck Avenue
White Plains, NY 10605
www.marchofdimes.com

National Association of Psychiatric Treatment Centers for Children
1025 Connecticut Ave. NW, Suite 1012
Washington, D.C. 20036
(202) 857-9735

Operation Smile
Craniofacial/cleft lip and palate
www.operationsmile.org

The Sensory Processing Disorder
SPD—The misinterpretation of the sense, touch sounds movement, etc.
www.sinetwork.org

Wide Smiles
Cleft lip and palate resource
www.widesmiles.org

Adoption Books

Where to Find Adoption Books

Adoptshoppe Books
www.adoptshoppebooks.com

Alphabet Soup Books
www.alphabetsoupbooks.com

EMK Press
Adoption Publishing Company
www.emkpress.com/index

Perspectives Press
Publishes books on infertility and adoption
www.PerspectivesPress.com

Tapestry Books
Mail-order catalog with books on adoption and parenting issues
www.tapestrybooks.com

Adoption and Parenting

Adoption Parenting: Creating a Toolbox, Building Connections
Edited by Jean MacLeod and Sheena Macrae, Ph.D.
EMK Press, 2006

The Adoption Resource Book
Lois Gilman
Perennial Library, 1987

Are Those Kids Yours? American Families with Children Adopted from Other Countries
Cheri Register, Ph.D.

Attaching in Adoption: Practical Tools for Today's Parent
Deborah D. Gray
Perspectives Press, 2001

The Complete Adoption Book
Laura Beauvais-Godwin and Raymond Godwin
Adams Media Corporation, 1997

The Handbook of International Adoption Medicine: A Guide for Physicians, Parents, and Providers.
Laurie C. Miller, M.D.
Oxford University Press, 2005

Inside Transracial Adoption
Gail Steinberg and Beth Hall

International Adoption: Challenges and Opportunities
Thais Tepper, Lois Hannon, and Dorothy Sandstrom (ed.)

Keys to Parenting an Adopted Child
Kathy Lancaster
Barron's Educational Services, Inc., 1996

Lifebooks: Creating a Treasure for the Adopted Child
Beth O'Malley
Adoption-Works, 2001

The Out of Sync Child: Recognizing and Coping with Sensory Integration Disorder
Carol Stock Kranowitz, M.A.

Parenting with Love and Logic
Foster Cline, M.D. and Jim Fay
Pinon Press, 1990

The Post-Adoption Blues: Overcoming the Unforeseen Challenges of Adoption
Karen J. Foli, PH.D and John R. Thompson, M.D.
Rodale Books, 2004

Raising Adopted Children
Lois Ruskai Melina
HarperCollins, 1998

Toddler Adoption: The Weaver's Craft
Mary Hopkins-Best
Perspectives Press, 1997

Twenty Things Adopted Kids Wish Their Adoptive Parents Knew
Sherrie Eldridge
Random House, 1999

With Eyes Wide Open: A Workbook for Parents Adopting International Children over Age One.
Margie Miller and Nancy Ward
LN Press, Incorporated, 1996

China Adoption Books

A Passage to the heart: Writings from Families with Children from China
Amy Klatzkin, Editor

Adoption Nation: Families with Children from China Edition
Adam Pertman

The Chinese Adoption Handbook: How to Adopt from China and Korea
John H. Maclean
Writers Club Press, 2003

Daughter from Afar: A Family's International Adoption Story
Sarah L. Woodard
Writers Club Press, 2002

International Adoption Travel Journal
Mary E. Petertyl

Intercountry Adoption from China: Examining the Cultural Heritage and Other Post-adoption Issues
Jay W. Rojewski, and Jacy L. Rojewski
Bergin & Garvey Paperback, 2001

The Lost Daughters of China: Abandoned Girl's, Their Journey to America, and the Search for a Missing Past
Karin Evans
Tarcher, 2001

The Waiting Child: How the Faith and Love of One Orphan Saved the Life of Another
Cindy Champnella
Yeong and Yeong Book Company, 2004

Wanting a Daughter, Needing a Son: Abandonment, Adoption, and Orphanage Care in China
Kay Ann Johnson, Any Klatzkin
Yeong and Yeong Book Company, 2004

Wuhu Diary: On taking My Adopted Daughter Back to her Hometown in China
Emily Prager
Random House, 2001

Miscellaneous
Adopting From China—A Video Survival Guide
Rebecca Coates Nee
ISBN B00006JIUP

Adoption Books for Children

At Home in this World: A China Adoption Story
Jean MacLeod

I Don't Have Your Eyes
Carrie Kitze

I love you like Crazy Cakes
Rose Lewis

Kids like me in China
Ying Ying Fry with Amy Klatzkin

Mommy Far, Mommy Near: An Adoption Story
Carol Antoinette Peacock

Shaoey and Dot
Marybeth and Steven Chapman

We See the Moon
Carrie Kitze

When You Were Born in China
Sara Dorow

Other Books

The American Academy of Pediatrics, The Complete and Authoritative Guide, Caring for Your Baby and Young Child, Birth to Age 5
Steven P. Shelov, MD, F.A.A.P., Editor-in-Chief
Bantam Books, 1998

The Baby Book, Everything You Need to Know about Your Baby-from Birth to Age Two.
William Sears, M.D. and Martha Sears, R.N.
Little Brown and Company, 1993

The Girlfriends Guide to Toddlers
Vickie Iovine
Penguin Putnam, 1999

The Pink and Blue Toddler and Preschooler Pages, Practical Tips and Advice for Parents
Laurie Waldstein and Leslie Zinberg
Contemporary Books, 1999

What to Expect, the Toddler Years
Arlene Eisenberg, Heidi E. Murkoff, and Sandee E. Hathaway, B.S. N.
Workman Publishing, 1996

Showers, the Complete Guide to Hosting a Perfect Bridal or Baby Shower
Beverly Clark
Wilshire Publications, 1989

Language and Travel Resources

Adopting from China, A Language and Parenting Guide
By Teresa Kelleher
Tender Loving Communications
P.O. Box 90
Taylor, AZ 85939-0090
http://worknotes.com/AZ/AdoptingFromRussia/Kelleher/hl.stm

Berlitz Passport to 31 Languages (CD-ROM)
Includes Chinese, Korean, Russian, Vietnamese, and more.
The Learning Company, Inc.
www.learningco.com

Chinese in 10 Minutes a Day
Kristine K. Kershul

Chinese (Mandarin) Instant Conversational Language-Mandarin Chinese
By Pimsleur

Lonely Planet China/Beijing

Lonely Planet Mandarin Phrasebook
Anthony Garnut

Travel—Frommer's China: The 50 Most Memorable Trips

Adoption-Related and Multicultural Gifts

A Mother's Charm
Sterling silver adoption charms, Sponsor of "The Adoption Journey" conferences
www.motherscharm.com

AdoptShoppe.com
Unique adoption gifts
www.adoptshoppe.com

AdoptionShop.com
www.adoptionshop.com

Asia for Kids
Language and culture resource; large selection of books, includes China, Vietnam, Korea, India, Russia, and more
www.asiaforkids.com

Celebrate the Child
Large selection of products from, China, Korea, Vietnam, Cambodia, and more
www.celebratechild.com

China Sprout
Chinese cultural products and services
www.chinasprout.com

References

Chapter1: Adopting From China

John H. Maclean, *The Chinese Adoption Handbook: How to Adopt from China and Korea* (Lincoln, NE, iUniverse, 2003).

Let's Travel in China, A Travel Press Book, Edited by Darlene Geis, 1965, Children's Press, Inc. Chicago.

"Rivers In China", www.china-window.com

Families with Children from China, "Known Holidays and Slow Periods in China," www.fwcc.org/packtips

"New Year Customs", www.Chinapictures.org

Jay W. Rojewski and Jacy L. Rojewski, Intercountry Adoption From China, Examining Cultural Heritage and Other Post Adoption Issues, (Westport, Connecticut, Bergin & Garvey, 2001).

"Climate of China", "Geography" www.TravelChinaGuide.com, 6/08-2005

Our Chinese Daughters Foundation, "How to Adopt", "Chinese Culture", "Travel To China", www.OCDF.org

BeijingTrip.Com, "Attractions: The Great Wall, Summer Palace, Tienamen Square", http://www.beijingtrip.com/attractions/greatwall/intro.htm

www.Wikipedia.org, "Beijing opera, Chinese Acrobats, Chinese Theatre" http://en.wikipedia.org/wiki/Beijing_opera

Chinese Holidays & Festivals, http://www.index-china.com/index-english/chinese_holidays.htm

www.About.com, Chinese Culture, http://chineseculture.about.com/library/weekly/aa052998.htm

Chapter 2: What's in a Name?

Deborah McCurdy, *Choosing a Name for Your Foreign-Born Child, Report on Intercountry Adoption 2000,* International Concerns for Children.

Chapter 3: Baby Showers and Gift Registry

Beverly Clark, *Showers, the Complete Guide to Hosting a Perfect Bridal or Baby Shower, Shower for an Adopted Baby* (Carpenteria, CA: Wilshire Publications, 1989).

Chapter 4: While You Are Waiting

John H. Maclean, *Russian Adoption Handbook: How to Adopt a Child from Russia, Ukraine and Kazakhstan,* (Lincoln, NE: Writers Club Press, 2000).

Chapter5: The Wardrobe

Cyndi Peck, "Packing Suggestions" www.AdoptionGuides.org

Chapter 6: The Nursery

William Sears, M.D.& Martha Sears, R.N., *The Baby Book* (Boston: Little, Brown & Company, 1993).

"Baby Registry Must Haves," Babies R Us, The Baby Superstore.

Arlene Eisenberg, Heidi E. Murkoff, and Sandee E. Hathaway, B.S.N., *What to Expect the Toddler Years* (New York: Workman Publishing, 1994).

Lois Ruskai Melina, *Raising Adopted Children: Practical Reassuring Advice for Every Adoptive Parent* (New York: HarperCollins Publishers, Inc., 1998).

Mary Hopkins-Best, *Toddler Adoption: The Weaver's Craft* (Indianapolis, IN: Perspectives Press, 1997).

John H. Maclean, *The Chinese Adoption Handbook: How to Adopt from China and Korea* (Lincoln, NE, iUniverse, 2003).

Chapter 7: The Toy Box

William Sears, M.D.& Martha Sears, R.N., *The Baby Book* (Boston: Little, Brown & Company, 1993).

Chapter 8: Child Safety

Steven P. Shelvov, M.D. and Robert E. Hannemann, M.D., *The American Academy of Pediatrics, Caring for Your Baby and Young Child—Birth to Age Five* (New York: Bantam Books, 1998).

"What You Should Know about Strollers, What You Should Know about Childproofing Your Home, What You Should Know about Baby Bath Time," USA Baby, May 14, 1999, www.babysroom.com

William Sears, M.D.& Martha Sears, R.N., *The Baby Book* (Boston: Little, Brown & Company, 1993).

Arlene Eisenberg, Heidi E. Murkoff, and Sandee E. Hathaway, B.S.N., *What to Expect the Toddler Years* (New York: Workman Publishing, 1994).

Chapter 9: A Safe Outdoors

Laurie Waldstein and Leslie Zinberg, *The Pink and Blue Toddler and Preschooler Pages—Practical Tips and Advice for Parents* (Lincolnwood, IL: Contemporary Books, 1999).

Arlene Eisenberg, Heidi E. Murkoff, and Sandee E. Hathaway, B.S.N., *What to Expect the Toddler Years* (New York: Workman Publishing, 1994).

Chapter 10: Mealtime Mania

Mary Hopkins-Best, *Toddler Adoption: The Weaver's Craft* (Indianapolis, IN: Perspectives Press, 1997).

Richard C. Theur, Ph.D., Infant Nutritionist and Vice President of Research and Development, Beech-Nut Nutrition Corporation, "Feeding Your Baby Right, Allergies, Microwaving, Water, Juices."

William Sears, M.D.& Martha Sears, R.N., *The Baby Book* (Boston: Little, Brown & Company, 1993).

John H. Maclean, *Russian Adoption Handbook: How to Adopt a Child from Russia, Ukraine and Kazakhstan,* (Lincoln, NE: Writers Club Press, 2000).

Toddler, Crawler, and Sitter Product, June 30, 1999, www.gerber.com

"Feeding Suggestions While Abroad", Deborah Borchers, MD, Families with Children from China, Child Feeding Suggestions.

Holly Van Gulden and Lisa M. Bartels-Rabb "Babies, A look at what to expect at different developmental stages of babyhood-and what each stage means for adoptive parents," www.AdoptiveFamilie.com, August 2005

Alla Gordina, MD, www.GlobalPediatrics.net

Chapter 11: Bath Time

John H. Maclean, *The Chinese Adoption Handbook: How to Adopt from China and Korea* (Lincoln, NE, iUniverse, 2003).

Chapter 12: Diaper Care and Potty Training

William Sears, M.D.& Martha Sears, R.N., *The Baby Book* (Boston: Little, Brown & Company, 1993).

Steven P. Shelvov, M.D. and Robert E. Hannemann, M.D., *The American Academy of Pediatrics, Caring for Your Baby and Young Child—Birth to Age Five* (New York: Bantam Books, 1998).

Chapter 13: The Medicine Cabinet

Arlene Eisenberg, Heidi E. Murkoff, and Sandee E. Hathaway, B.S.N., *What to Expect the Toddler Years* (New York: Workman Publishing, 1994).

Steven P. Shelvov, M.D. and Robert E. Hannemann, M.D., *The American Academy of Pediatrics, Caring for Your Baby and Young Child—Birth to Age Five* (New York: Bantam Books, 1998).

Chapter 14: The Pediatrician

Steven P. Shelvov, M.D. and Robert E. Hannemann, M.D., *The American Academy of Pediatrics, Caring for Your Baby and Young Child—Birth to Age Five* (New York: Bantam Books, 1998).

William Sears, M.D.& Martha Sears, R.N., *The Baby Book* (Boston: Little, Brown & Company, 1993).

Dr. Dana Johnson, M.D., Ph.D., "International Adoption: New Kids, New Challenges, Evaluation after Arrival, Screening Tests, Immunizations."

"Is Your Child Sick?" The Alliance for South Carolina's Children, Columbia, S.C.

Chapter 15: Medical Considerations for Adopted Children

William Sears, M.D.& Martha Sears, R.N., *The Baby Book* (Boston: Little, Brown & Company, 1993).

Lois Ruskai Melina, *Raising Adopted Children: Practical Reassuring Advice for Every Adoptive Parent* (New York: HarperCollins Publishers, Inc., 1998).

Lois Gilman, *The Adoption Resource Book,* 3rd ed. (New York: HarperCollins Publishers, 1992).

Mary Hopkins-Best, *Toddler Adoption: The Weaver's Craft* (Indianapolis, IN: Perspectives Press, 1997).

Dr. Jane Aronson "An Update on Health Issues in Children Adopted From China", www.OrphanDoctor.com

"Please Talk to Me, A Speech Guide for Parents," South Carolina Department of Health and Environmental Control, 9/02.

"How Do You Know if Your Child Needs Extra Help in School?" The Stargazer, Newsletter for the Dr. William R. DeLoache Center for Developmental Services, Greenville, South Carolina, fall, 2004.

"Mongolian Spots—-Did you tell the sitter?", China Connection, June/July, 1996.

Chapter 16: Child-care, Preschool, and Babysitters

Steven P. Shelvov, M.D. and Robert E. Hannemann, M.D., *The American Academy of Pediatrics, Caring for Your Baby and Young Child—Birth to Age Five* (New York: Bantam Books, 1998).

Mary Hopkins-Best, *Toddler Adoption: The Weaver's Craft* (Indianapolis, IN: Perspectives Press, 1997).

William Sears, M.D.& Martha Sears, R.N., *The Baby Book* (Boston: Little, Brown & Company, 1993).

Laurie Waldstein and Leslie Zinberg, *The Pink and Blue Toddler and Preschooler Pages—Practical Tips and Advice for Parents* (Lincolnwood, IL: Contemporary Books, 1999).

"Baby Sitting Reminders," the American Academy of Pediatrics, Tip, The Injury Prevention Program, (1994).

Chapter 17: International Adoption

Laurie Waldstein and Leslie Zinberg, *The Pink and Blue Toddler and Preschooler Pages—Practical Tips and Advice for Parents* (Lincolnwood, IL: Contemporary Books, 1999).

Russia-Consular Information Sheet, January 19, 1999, www.travel.state.gov

Dr. Jane Aronson "Immunizations for Families Going Abroad for Inter-country Adoption," June 12, 2000, www.OrphanDoctor.com

"Travel and Vacations, Child Safety Seats on Airplanes, Choosing the Correct Child Safety Restraint for Air Travel, Tips for Flying with a Child," May 14, 1999, www.Parenting-qa.com

John H. Maclean, *Russian Adoption Handbook: How to Adopt a Child from Russia, Ukraine and Kazakhstan,* (Lincoln, NE: Writers Club Press, 2000).

Consular Information Sheet, May 28, 2005, U.S. Department of State, Bureau of Consular Affairs, Washington, DC 20520.

Chapter 18: Packing For Your Trip

Laurie Waldstein and Leslie Zinberg, *The Pink and Blue Toddler and Preschooler Pages—Practical Tips and Advice for Parents* (Lincolnwood, IL: Contemporary Books, 1999).

Eldon C. Romney, "Packing for Travel to Russia," Eastern European Adoption Coalition, July 6, 1999, www.eeadopt.com

Dr. Jane Aronson, "Preparation for Travel to Another Land," July 16, 2000, www.OrphanDoctor.com

"What to Wear on the Trip of a Lifetime," Travel Tips by Tree of Life Adoption Center, June 11, 1999, www.toladopt.org

John H. Maclean, *The Chinese Adoption Handbook: How to Adopt from China and Korea* (Lincoln, NE, iUniverse, 2003).

Chapter 19: While You Are There

Laurie Waldstein and Leslie Zinberg, *The Pink and Blue Toddler and Preschooler Pages—Practical Tips and Advice for Parents* (Lincolnwood, IL: Contemporary Books, 1999).

"Gift Giving," Travel Tips by Tree of Life Adoption Center, June 11, 1999, www.toladopt.org

Chapter 20:Meeting your Daughter

Jay W. Rojewski and Jacy L. Rojewski, *Intercountry Adoption From China, Examining Cultural Heritage and Other Post Adoption Issues,* (Westport, Connecticut, Bergin & Garvey, 2001).

Dr. Jane Aronson, "Lili's Story—Hale and Hardy Chinese Orphans" April, 14,2004, 2000, www.OrphanDoctor.com

Our Chinese Daughters Foundation, "Travel To China" www.OCDF.org

Dr. George Rogu, "Physican: Post-Institutional Rehabilitative Strategies," April 25, 2006, www.International.Adoption.com

Lynne Lyon, MSW, LSW, "Attachment and Bonding", www.Attach-China.org

Cyndi Peck, "Packing Suggestions," www.AdoptionGuides.org

Chapter 21: Home Sweet Home

John H. Maclean, *Russian Adoption Handbook: How to Adopt a Child from Russia, Ukraine and Kazakhstan,* (Lincoln, NE: Writers Club Press, 2000).

Harriet McCarthy, "Post Adoption Depression, The Unacknowledged Hazard," PAD Survey, Eastern European Adoption Coalition, 2000.

June Bond, "Post-Adoption Depression Syndrome," *Roots and Wings* 6 no.4 (Spring 1995).

Jessica Brooke-Buskirk, Top 10 Ways to Culturally Connect your Child. Adoption Today, June/July 2006.

10 Great Ways to Introduce Birth Culture to your Adopted Child, Cultural Care Au Pair, www.culturecare.com

Joan N. Ramos, M.S.W., Understanding Race and Adoption, Adoption Today, February/March 2004.

Jay W. Rojewski and Jacy L. Rojewski, *Intercountry Adoption From China, Examining Cultural Heritage and Other Post Adoption Issues,* (Westport, Connecticut, Bergin & Garvey, 2001).

C.J. Lyford, Esquire, "Readoption-What is it? Do you need to do it, Should you do it? What Does it Involve?, Some things to consider regarding readoption," www.fwcc.org

Gail Steinberg and Beth Hall, What is Transracial Adoption?, EMK Press, 2003.

About the Author

Denise Harris Hoppenhauer is an Adoptive Parent and Adoption Advocate. *She is the Author of Adopting A Toddler: What Size Shoes Does She Wear?* and has had numerous adoption-related articles published in variety of medium.

She is a founding member of the South Carolina Adoption Coalition for Education and Support (ACES). Denise teaches pre-adoption education courses and is a post adoption support group leader. She was the 2003 recipient of the Dave Thomas Award from the South Carolina Council on Adoptable Children.

She lives in Greenville, South Carolina with her husband Michael, their children Callie and Sean, and cat Max.

Denise is the Executive Director of *Adobaby, LLC*. She can be reached at Bunny@theHopps.com

978-0-595-41523-6
0-595-41523-7